CW01647577

SKETCHES:

AN ANTHOLOGY OF ESSAYS, ART, AND POETRY

Joseph C. Zinker

Edited and with a Forward
by Paul Shane

Copyright © 2001 by Joseph C. Zinker.

All rights reserved. No part of this publication may be reproduced, stored in a retrieval system, or transmitted, in any form or by any means, electronic, mechanical, photocopying, recording, or otherwise without the prior written permission of the publisher.

Published by: The GestaltPress
66 Orchard Street
Cambridge, MA 02140

Distributed by: The Analytic Press, Inc., Hillsdale, NJ.

Apperceptive Mass: My Grounding originally appeared in *The Gestalt Journal*, Spring, 1980.

Searching for Clarity originally appeared in *Pilgrimage*, 11(2), 1983.

The Therapist As Artist originally appeared as "Creative Process in Gestalt Therapy: The Therapist as Artist" as a Gestalt Institute of Cleveland monograph in 1974.

Synthetic Thinking originally appeared in *Body Process* by James I. Kepner, Jossey-Bass Publishers, 1986/1993. Reprinted with permission of the publisher.

Phenomenology of the Here and Now originally appeared as a Gestalt Institute of Cleveland monograph in 1973.

On Grandparently Love originally appeared in *Voices*, 12(4), 1976/1977.

Polemics, Systems and the Nature of Interventions was originally presented at the Seventh British Gestalt Conference at Cambridge University, July 1, 1993.

Excerpts from Rosa Lee was drawn from *Rosa Lee: Motivation and the Crisis of Dying*, Volume VI, Lake Erie College Studies, 1966.

Entitlement: A Meditation for the Psychotherapy Patient originally appeared in *The Psychotherapy Patient*, 1985, The Haworth Press. Reprinted with permission of the publisher.

In Search of a Therapeutic Eclecticism originally appeared in *Voices*, 16(3), 1980.

Discussions with the Masters originally appeared in *Gestalt Therapy Discussions with the Masters*, 1990, Charles C. Thomas Publisher. Reprinted with permission of the author.

Interview with Joseph C. Zinker by Clive Hierons is reprinted with permission of the author.

Lies in Intimate Systems originally appeared in the *Center for the Study of Intimate Systems News*, 1(2), 1981.

Why Children? originally appeared in the *Center for Intimate Systems News*, 4(1), 1984.

Marriage: The Impossible Relationship originally appeared in the *Center for Intimate Center News*, 5(1), 1985.

Cover painting, "Brooklyn in Dark Colors," by Joseph C. Zinker, 1950.
Cover and interior design by Tom Canale, Canale Studios.
Graphics photography by Wendell Price.
Back cover photograph by Reginald Hunt.

ISBN 0-88163-339-9

For Sandra Regina

Contents

Contents

Forward
Pieces of a Mosaic

Readers will enjoy the present anthology--*Sketches*--by Joseph Zinker for many different reasons. The most compelling reason is that it gives an intimate view into the professional, personal, and artistic minds of a proven master therapist and teacher in a very unusual mixture of content and format. It does so through a selection of his early essays interspersed with poems, drawings, and paintings. This makes the book especially engaging in that it differs markedly from his previous two works--*Creative Process in Gestalt Therapy* (1977) and *In Search of Good Form* (1994)--both very fine efforts in their own rights--but Sketches is an altogether different animal. You will find among its pages a subtle blend of professional thoughts and musings sprinkled with art and poetic meditations. While the main portion of its subject matter is reflections on the practice of psychotherapy, it is not a "professional" book on the topic. While it is littered with Joseph's drawings and poetry, it is not an anthology of reproduced prints and drawings. Neither is it a book of poetry. It's none of those things and yet it contains the best qualities of all three. It's an artistic work demonstrating how art and psychotherapy work may be blended into an aesthetic whole of a life of work

The reader will also find this book remarkable in that it is so very intimate. Joseph gives the reader glimpses into his mind and heart, giving insights into his life and thought in many ways and on many different levels. Perhaps a glimpse will come from a trenchant remark found in one of the essays; perhaps it will stand out in a line of poetry; perhaps in the lines of a drawing.

This book deserves extended study in and of itself because of the significance of Joseph's influence in Gestalt therapy and its lineage extending back to European depth psychology. Given that my own graduate studies have been in the history and philosophy of psychology, I cannot help but to frame Zinker's work within a historical and philosophical context. As I have commented elsewhere, Zinker's main contribution to Gestalt therapy and the existential depth tradition has been as the latest evolutionary link in a chain extending from Paul Goodman and Fritz Perls back to Karl Jaspers (Shane, 1998).

That is, Jaspers, as the modern father of existentialism, coined the concept of the *Grenzsituation*. This term has been translated in a variety of ways including "boundary situation," "limit situation," or, as Goodman knew it in Gestalt Therapy, the "extreme situation" (Perls, Hefferline, & Goodman, 1951, p. 324). Goodman used the term without attribution because it was an idea that was "in the air" at the time as existential philosophy began invading bohemian intellectual circles in the late 1940s. Conceptually, the extreme situation is the philosophical inspiration for that most marvelous of all oxymorons, the "experimental safe emergency." The confrontation with the *Grenzsituation* according to Jaspers leads to the experience of *Existenz*, an experience functionally identical with Perls's aim of using therapy to awaken one's "sense of actuality" (Perls, 1947/1969). It becomes in the 1951 text a technical cornerstone of Gestalt therapy: the creation of a moment of crisis in the form of an experiment.

As opposed to concentrating solely on the actual situation and waiting for gestalt completion at some critical mass point in awareness as Goodman recommends or mechanically directing the client step-by-step to an impasse point as does Perls, Zinker makes the experiment into a collaborative effort, a shared experience, and a spontaneously evolving act of creative energy; one that is aimed at a goal to be sure, but also one that is open-ended in outcome.

Zinker's legacy is to have transformed the Gestalt experiment with language, images, principles and values embodied in the aesthetic. His project has been both aesthetic and epistemological in nature. What helps one achieve this fundamental shift in aesthetic vision is based, in part, on the therapist's presence and his or her ability to make phenomenological observations about process rather than content. It is for this reason that Joseph often facetiously describes himself as being merely "a process junkie."

Forward

The idea for this book came about a few short years ago at the GestaltPress with the original intention to present some of the lesser-known essays by Joseph. The project began with the rather amorphous plan of featuring a group of essays along with reproductions of Joseph's art and poetry that would give the reader a more intimate glimpse into Joseph's thought and work than a standard psychotherapy text. Our reasoning was to introduce the reader not only to the trajectory of Joseph's conceptual thought over the course of his career while also displaying Joseph's aesthetic creativity as it is such an integral part of his perspective. If there is one unifying thread to Joseph's work it is the incorporation of the creative act in all of its manifestations: in painting and drawing, in writing, in therapy, in living.

That was pretty much all we followed as a blueprint and the book has been growing organically for more than a year since that time. The process of its growth has been quite interesting to witness as it has been marked with unexpected and often happy events. For example, Joseph collected materials over the months finding them here and there to eventually fill a large file folder bulging with old journal articles. Then came more articles found in the odd file cabinet and unopened carton in his basement. Then a pack of black-and-white line drawings was found. During the course of this collecting, a close friend of Joseph's--Wendell Price--brought to our attention some old paintings and drawings given to him by Joseph some years ago--some even reaching back to Joseph's childhood in 1950s Brooklyn, New York. Color slides of paintings, old scraps of poetic scribbling, lecture notes, framed pieces of art… many things turned up for reading, remembering, contemplation, discussion, selection, and rejection.

Slowly, like a plant gradually rising and unfolding its leaves one at a time, the book began taking shape. Many past articles and paintings were reviewed, but only a few were chosen for various editorial reasons. The standards of selection used were quite simple: select only the best, the most representative of Joseph's work, and what would be best graphically reproduced. It was our collective intention from the beginning to let the material ultimately dictate its own organization. As I look at the book as a whole, as a Gestalt, I experience a parade of images, ideas, and insights that are all uniquely

Joseph's. I see that all of the things that we selected have come together in such a way as to feel that each of them was "just right" for this project. My experience, as I feel it, is also punctuated by impressions and feelings of things I've known about Joseph personally, having been a friend and colleague for more than a decade, but also by other things that I had not known. That is, in one way I have heard Joseph discuss some of the ideas contained here either in conversation or in a lecture and so they resonate with me as being known. In another way, however, especially in Joseph's poetry, he gives his feelings, some of them painfully raw, and so he draws my heart even closer. In this regard, for me, this book holds a feeling of being in the presence of something familiar, yet I still find things among its pages that continue to surprise and delight me everytime I open it. This book is much like my friend and teacher, Joseph: a source of friendly warmth and comfort, shrewd insights and hard-won wisdom, playful humor, as well as the novel, the deadly serious, and the thought-provoking. On behalf of the GestaltPress, I sincerely hope that the reader will take as much pleasure in enjoying the many different pieces in this anthology as we have in assembling them--like a mosaic--into a finished, and aesthetic whole.

Paul Shane *Brecksville, Ohio*
February 13, 2001

References

Perls, F. (1947/1969). *Ego, hunger, and aggression: The beginning of gestalt therapy.* New York, NY: Vintage Books.

Perls, F., Hefferline, R., & Goodman, P. (1951). *Gestalt therapy: Excitement and growth in the human personality.* New York, NY: Julian Press.

Shane, P. (1998). *Of straw men, Dr. Pangloss, and the evolution of the safe emergency: A critique.* Australian Gestalt Journal, 2(1).

what is right?
what is wrong?
Its scary
to receive
love-
"surrender"

Acknowledgements

First of all, I want to thank Gordon Wheeler not only for inviting me to create this anthology but for his constant presence in recent years as on advocate of my writing and my creative work. My editor, Paul Shane, lived with the creation of *In Search of Good Form* and now with the careful editorial construction of writings and images in this book.

I thank Sonia Nevis and Edwin Nevis for the interviews at the end of the book. Sonia's ideas have always been helpful in my writing. A good friend's thinking is not always easy to hear and accept, but a wise man is one who listens well. Honesty between friends can hurt deeply; can infuriate--but also adds "muscle" to our formulations about life.

I thank colleagues who interviewed me: Irving Bailin, Robert Harman, and Clive Hierons.

I am indebted to those publishers who cooperated in the reprinting of my past works and who have supported me in this and other projects such as my friend and often-time publisher, Joe Wysong.

I am grateful to my mentors: Fritz and Laura Perls, Erving Polster, Carl Whitaker, Abraham Maslow, and Dwight Miles--also, my art teachers at the Brooklyn Museum, Moses and Raphael Soyer--they were teachers who gave with the joy born of their own inspiration and creative generosity. I am grateful for the generosity and support of my colleagues around the world.

Finally, I want to acknowledge the kind and patient help of my dear wife Sandra Regina and that of my daughters, Judith and Karen. Special thanks to my friend Wendell Price who held on to the art I tried to throw out and who photographed much of my work for the present volume.

Joseph Zinker *Wellfleet, Massachusetts*
January 5, 2001

1992

Preface

Dear Reader,

Here is a collection of some works I have produced during the last thirty-eight years. They include my thoughts about therapeutic eclecticism, the nature of presence, how polemics, and systems influence interventions in psychotherapy, and synthetic thinking. Over the years I've been fascinated by synectics, the nature of pattern formation in the physical world. In my travels around the world I have again fallen in love with Chagall, Picasso, the poetry of Neruda, the ancient streets of Malta and Jerusalem, the music of Mozart, Beethoven, and Villa-Lobos. Every artistic experience fired my interest in bringing my work closer to the arts.

In my first major work, *Creative Process in Gestalt Therapy*, I explored the relationship of the creative impulse and how it affects the elegance of psychotherapy... For me, the magic moment of any creation emerges in the thickened space between two or more human beings. In Gestalt therapy, we call it "contact," but contact does not begin to describe the powerful process of experiencing the beauty of another human being, experiencing the pathos of our daily struggle to survive, to play, to love. In the film, "Life is Beautiful," we see how the most awful aspects of human cruelty can connect with the sweet innocence of a little boy and a grown man's ability to magically transform his life, so as to save the boy's life... I was such a boy...in the Second World War in Europe; while sitting in a cathedral basement, where everyone was worried to death--I managed to transform my fright to focusing on the beautiful fabric of my mother's dress. It quieted me. This was happening while my father and brother were outside in the streets of Lutzk burying fallen corpses. This was a moment of transformation of an eight-year-old boy. For the following 20 years, I struggled with my nightmares of being chased by Nazis. At the same time, I continued drawing and painting. By age 18, I spoke Russian, Polish, English, Yiddish, some German, and a little Hebrew. I wrote poetry in Yiddish and Russian in the displaced persons camps in Germany. I was reinventing myself and the world around me. Years later, I wrote a doctoral dissertation on the dying process of an African-American woman so as to ease my death phobias. Psychotherapy with psychoanalysts and, most importantly, with Erving Polster helped me to be less frightened and to move forward as a husband and a father.

Still, I paid a heavy price for my experiences, a basically post-traumatic person. I didn't know how to be a friend, how to be generous, how to really give and receive...all this happened while I managed to be a psychotherapist. I was able to be outrageously creative and, on occasions felt as if I was performing miracles with my clients. But sadly, I have made mistakes and the enormous pain of my regret has muted all self-congratulatory statements of my successes. As a wise friend of mine told me, "In the final analysis, one's woundedness is ultimately a source of strength, but there is always the presence of the shadow polarity to be reckoned with, and for this, one can never escape responsibility."

The sense of being thrilled as well as feeling suicidal is expressed in several of the poems in the book. Yet, somehow, the sensation of loving and being loved saved me. My soul and my heart are deeply scarred. But, I am alive.

Several interviews in this book show how I managed to connect with friends and colleagues. Slowly, I learned to feel joyful about the learning process with my peers.

As I page through the book I see a painting by a 16-year-old boy of desolate Brooklyn buildings with "empty eyes." Yet, the longing for color and the yearning for beauty come through... I see an idealized man's face... and another face, loose and relaxed with a note about surrender. Then I see a recent Japanese calligraphy that has enormous power and integrity... another idealized drawing of a face with a diagram of a heart in his chest. I see a drawing of a man with horrendously frightened eyes and an image of a frightened mother with her child... and more.

I have opened my soul especially in these drawings and many of the poems.

In my life, I have fought hard to look ahead and to look forward to walk serenely in front of my Cape Cod cottage hand in hand with my wife, my daughters, and my friends. Today I am writing this for you with complete transparency. A full life is replete with hurts, regrets, mistakes and also victories and thrilling discoveries. I have never felt so real, complete, and rich as I feel today. I am able to bear having been irreparably damaged, to have disappointed myself and others. This is the paradox of being broken and complete at the same time.

I am an old man with arthritis and a collection of pills. But at night I retire with someone who saved my life, saved my soul... A blessing.

And so I offer you these little productions in the hope that some of them will touch your minds and hearts.

Enjoy.

Joseph Zinker

Wellfleet, Massachusetts
May 2001

contact
Meyer Zimmer 1976

The creative intention is a yearning in one's body,
    a desire to fill the container of life.
This yearning expresses itself in energy, movement,
    rhythm.
The activity of creation, its expression, is a loving
    assertion of life.
Creation is an act of thankfulness or an act of cursing.
It is the privilege of tasting seeing, touching life,
    a celebration of being
    or a pleading for a meaningful exit.

J.Z., 1/1/76

1

Apperceptive Mass: My Grounding

Spring 1980

Psychotherapy does not take place in a vacuum. It is not "layed on" another person. Rather, it is a dynamic interaction between at least two people. One person is the specialist, the therapist, the counselor; the other is the client, a person in need, a fellow traveler. The creative process emerges from the interaction between the inner lives of these two people.

As therapists, we pay a great deal of attention to where the client comes from, but little to where we come from. Many reduce this question to a discussion of the relative merits of medical training versus training in pastoral counseling, clinical psychology, or psychiatric social work. A number of my colleagues have written elegant articles on educational methods, supervision, and theoretical and practical requirements of advanced training programs for therapists.

But a discussion of training provides only a partial view of a therapist's background. Some years ago, while working in Curacao, I asked a group of professionals to evaluate their formal education. A bright and sensitive Englishman pointed out that, although he had received adequate training, his education was abominable. He explained this discrepancy by describing training as the learning of basic tools for acquiring knowledge--the mechanics of mathematics, reading, writing. The goal of education, as he described it, is an appreciation of our own lives and the lives of others, and a sensitivity to and understanding of the events around us. It is a subtle process through which we create a rich tapestry of our lives.

This distinction between training and education is a significant one. A therapist cannot be defined merely by the school in which s/he received professional training or by the degree earned. No seasoned therapist uses a particular methodology as a repetitive formula. S/he takes ownership of some parts and rejects those that don't fit his/her experience; s/he experiments with a technique, modifying it to his/her style. The methodology is molded by the therapist's unique working characteristics: depth or shallowness, discipline or looseness, awareness or dullness, liveliness or cautiousness, spontaneity or conservatism, expansiveness or stinginess, creativity or constriction.

The therapist is, first and foremost, a person involved in lives. My concern here is with the therapist as a person. I address this issue by using myself as a subject to tell "where I come from" in the broadest sense of that expression. Against this personal ground, the reader may get a clearer figure, a sharper image of the origin and development of my work and the experiences I see as central to my perception of others.

When I was very young, my father, a dentist, had an office in our home. I was there with him since I could walk, always watching and listening. When he talked to people, he was animated and excited. I remember how warmly he related to people. My image is of a soft, personable man, as well as an excellent craftsman. My father cared for his patients. He loved repairing their ailing teeth or creating new ones for them. Most of all, he enjoyed the presence of people in his life; that was gravy, for him.

My father happened to make his livelihood as a mender of teeth. What I witnessed in his presence was a teacher who gave of his own experience, his presence to others: "Mrs. Matz," he would say, "if I remove the bumps from your denture, you will have no pain but the plate will fall out of your mouth. You must learn to stay with discomfort to make that denture part of your body. Sometimes there are rewards growing out of discomfort." If Mrs. Matz continued complaining, he would tell her a joke or a story to make his point stronger, relieving her pain with laughter.

As Sheldon Kopp (1971) put it: "So too with the psychotherapist, the significant part of what is therapeutic is not just the knowledge, strategies, or reinforcement schedules that he brings to the hour but the way in which he can be with the patient. When the therapist is himself and acts on what he feels, he is therapeutic... it is willingness to surrender to the compelling qualities of his experience of the patient" (p. 40). My father gave with abandon everything he valued in himself.

My mother still has presence. When she enters a room full of people, she communicates a regal stateliness. People turn and look. She is able to support herself silently. I feel that a therapist often communicates a profound message out of presence, what s/he radiates to others just by being in the world. The most important people in my life spoke to me with their silences.

I can see each of these strands in me now: the charm and drama of my mother, the way with people that my father has, and some of my brother's clever manipulativeness which I trimmed down to a size just right for my conscience.

But I was also different: the skinny kid, the quiet one. I was not pushed to become accomplished as my older brother was. When my parents and brother fought, I sat in the corner crying. The intensity of my feelings overwhelmed me and I began to find some comfort in solitude. Later in life, I found the need to study in solitude. Emerging out of such aloneness made me feel present for others. Looking back, I realize that in those early days of childhood I taught myself a form of meditation and self-support.

Aside from my immediate family, Wolf Klimburd was an important person in my early life. He was a physician friend of the family who saved my life during the war. He was another model of what it is to be a caring healer. Wolf took me into the labs of his hospital and showed me what a microscope looked like and how to identify blood cells. Wolf was a kind and gentle teacher. He attended to me; he cared for me.

No matter where we lived or what horrendous circumstances we lived through, I experienced caring, loyalty and love from those important people around me. I particularly recall one event in which we were on a highway in a truck transporting refugees. German planes were flying directly overhead and machine-gunning us at close range. My father grabbed hold of me and threw himself off the truck, rolling down the embankment with me in his arms. I heard him praying out loud as we were rolling down the hill, and I remember feeling enveloped by his power.

I don't know if there is a philosophical statement here other than I felt it was better to have been through the nightmare of the war knowing the love and courage of my parents than to have been isolated from the war and separated from the passion for life, which my parents taught me. This powerful attitude toward life is not unlike the more condensed process of creativity: it takes passion and courage to explode the ordinary situation and put it together in a brand new configuration.

Born and raised in Poland, the war became my life between the ages of seven and eleven. Then we were sent to refugee camps in Austria and Germany. I remember drawing in camp, taking an ORT course in electromechanics. I learned how to wire an electric motor; there were hundreds of bombed-out buildings and one could rewire the whole place for practice. ORT, a school organized by Jews in the Warsaw ghetto, was still operating to help refugees in camps after the war. Here I learned to speak and write Yiddish; I also learned some German. I loved to write and draw and I remember writing fairly fluent compositions in Russian and Yiddish. I thought I would become an electrical engineer; then, when I started studying the mathematical and mechanical subjects, I knew it was not for me. That was my training. Here is some of my education.

Image: I am visiting Wolf at the hospital. Looking through a window, I watch a woman in labor. I can see her separated legs and the head of an infant emerging from her body, just the beginning of the head coming out of her. It is a powerful, crisp image as I stand looking up, watching another life begin. Then a nurse notices me and chases me away.

The image of birth, of metamorphosis, is still very strong in me. I feel that all of us are in some ways helping or hindering each other's process of becoming, of coming more fully into the world.

Image: We are in a church basement. Our homes are being bombed. A woman with wild, staring eyes is screaming, "They are coming, here they are, they are coming..." over and over again.

At the age of six I began to wonder about justice and fairness, about our inhumanity to each other. And I was frightened. I realized then how human beings torture each other, how we drive each other crazy. The image and the thought still weigh me down.

Image: I am in a train full of refugees. We are stopped at a depot, surrounded by other trains. We are all very hungry. We sit, our legs handing out of the openings of the large open doors of cattle cars, staring out of tiredness and fright. Suddenly a nurse emerges from a military hospital train, and she is carrying a large tray of food. All the children run toward her. At closer range, I realize that the "goodies" on the tray are half-eaten chunks of moldy bread. We grab and eat. Our parents weep.

I learned compassion with my body--from the pains in a child's stomach.

Image: We enter Maidanek, a concentration camp in Poland. The Germans have just departed. The ovens are filled with ashes and bones. I see a small mound of baby shoes. Falling on my knees, I cry.

Image: We have paid the communist guards to let us cross the border from Poland to Czechoslovakia. It is night. A shot rings out, and a boy my own age falls dead next to me. We drag him to a nearby shack. I spend the night next to his body.

Image: While on an errand to buy ice cream, I see two Russian soldiers standing near a movie marquee in post-war Poland. I overhear one saying to the other that they don't have enough money to see the show. I use the ice cream money to buy two tickets. I approach them, hand them the tickets and walk away.

Image: In post-war Germany, I manage to get out of the camp gates to explore a local Bavarian village. German children run after me, yelling, "You dirty Jew!" I turn on them. They run away.

Image: We are in camp. I am turning 13. My father encourages me to study for my bar mitzvah. I answer, "A chosen people does not celebrate bar mitzvahs in camps. I will not do it." I still have the phylacteries my father gave me. My parents understood my dismay and respected my decision.

I have many images of sudden partings and tearful reunions.

They pass through me in slow motion: I am running toward my parents with open arms. Running and running.

I was pounded by my perceptions and sensitivities and almost overwhelmed by what I saw and by the nightmares that followed. I felt frightened and alone. At the same time, I grew to understand my own humanness.

The good years came--with America, art studios, college, travel, museums, etc. Years later I came into my profession with an apperceptive mass: an accumulated grounding of information and experience that seasoned my life. I am sharing with you isolated glimpses of the critical events in my life. I am not telling you that those particular experiences are the "true" prerequisites to becoming a person; rather, I use them as examples of the sort of experience, which has enriched me. It is important to have lived a life that has tested one's range of feeling.

As a teacher of therapists, I learned a long time ago that, although I can teach someone to acquire a sense of the history of psychotherapy, its concepts and methodology, I cannot teach someone to be a person. Even in those programs in which there is a personal psychotherapy requirement for one or more years, one may help a person resolve many unfinished situations and neurotic difficulties, but it is questionable whether one can teach the kind of fullness of being which evolves in a lifetime. Nevertheless, the depth of a therapy experience can have a profound effect on one's work as a helper, a healer.

I had two very powerful and varied therapy experiences: weekend sessions with Fritz Perls from 1959 until he died, and six years of regular therapy with Erv Polster. I learned very different things from these two men.

I learned the value of creative aloofness from Fritz. I discovered a place inside me, which has a rocklike quality and an insulation from the other person's presentation of self. This outlook helps me envision the person in ways s/he is unable to see for her/himself. Another, part of my aloofness is the effort, although not always successful, to focus and confront what the other person is communicating to me without swallowing his/her message whole.

I experienced Fritz as heartlessly uncompromising in his work with me. When I was on the other side of Fritz, I was frightened and felt misunderstood and shocked. I was often unaware of my learnings until much later. Yet I was moved by the sharpness of his scalpel and his piercing sensitivity. There are times when I can enter that part of myself and use my incisiveness and power.

Erv stimulated my Anima, my archetypal female, touching the other side of the polarity, which Fritz stimulated in me. And because Erv worked with me at the same time, I was able to move back and forth on that continuum from hardness to softness. My Anima is the ocean inside of me, the primordial mother. I carry her when I am with my family, friends and people in general. I feel her in the presence of animals and trees, flowers and grass. A flowing within me vibrates with nature; in those moments I am able to be quiet and reverent.

Erv saw me as a promising therapist; his vision of me reinforced my creative efforts. I felt his savoring of me. If he had an image of me hanging from a string, I was able to work with that image, relax my shoulders, be a puppet, and move into my lightness and dance. He was pleased that I was able to adventure him that way. Erv reinforced my liveliness and imagination.

Quite aside from his enormous sensitivity and understanding of me, I experienced Erv as Mother Earth.There were periods of three to four months when I didn't do anything in therapy. Erv hung in there with me. It is clear that he had great faith in the process of our work, and so did I. This makes me think about Fritz's impatience. I felt as if Fritz was always rushed with me, and it is nice to have had that kind of balance between being driven on the one hand, and being able to sit back and meditate on the other.

So the Anima part of me became more conscious in my work with Erv. It is the part of me that is loving, patient, and motherly. Not motherly in the chicken-soup sense, but in an acceptance of everything that is human in all of us. I trust the process of life and the process of my work with people.

I learned from Erv to be aware of the ocean inside of me, and Fritz connected me to my lightening. I learned to dip into a greater range of substance in myself, to find my individuality. I remember myself before therapy as, in some ways, fearful about public appearances, phobic about death, and quietly rigid. At that time my charisma came out with women; women "permitted" me to lean into my liveliness, excitement and my celebration of self and of life.

Before I was in therapy, my aliveness had a phony overlay, a hysterical quality. I would get easily excited and full of rhetoric. I was diffused and unclear rather than pointed, solidified and physically grounded. That brand of liveliness was not useful to me, other than as an announcement of good intentions--I promised more than I could deliver. In therapy I became aware of how I was compromising, confluent, and how I kissed ass just to be accepted and approved of. I learned to focus my excitement, to support myself with clarity of ideas, and to experience a sense of quietness underneath.

That fundamental groundedness came from a number of sources, not just from Erv and Fritz. My friends have always reinforced this process in me. But Fritz ruthlessly attacked my confluence. He made fun of me and belittled me whenever I showed any form of manipulation or obsequiousness. Also, he could not stand my righteousness.

I still cling to my righteousness and, in some situations, I value it. Fritz called me a rabbi, and there are times when I do feel like a spiritual guide, a gentle soul. At other times, I sound like a little old man who has the answers and is patting himself on the head for having them. I know I turn people off when I do that. But there are times when my righteousness directs me in making sound judgments.

I feel that, in a sense, the therapist is a testimonial person for his client. He says, "Yes" to the person's feelings, ideas, and characteristics that ought to be valued, but haven't been because circumstances in his client's life have not supported those qualities. I felt affirmed by my mother, but I needed affirmation from men. My therapists were all men, and what I received from them was an affirmation of certain manly qualities in me.

In many ways, therapy made it possible for me to focus on and develop already existing qualities, such as my romanticism and warmth. But I had no sense of my toughness. I had no sense of my power. I was like a little bird who could fly fast, was very durable, and could do many tricks in the air; but I had no experience of the barracuda in me, the panther, the Lear jet in me. Now I can move in very quickly and penetrate someone without being sadistic. The response from the other person is often a grateful, "You clever bastard!"

There was another thing I learned from Erv. He could take something that I presented as a "symptom" and make it possible for me to experience it as a support system. If I said, "I am sick and tired of my rigidity", he would get me into walking rigidly or thinking about my rigidity as a scholar. I was also able to get in touch with how my rigidity took care of me and how it failed. I did not feel compelled to give up all of it. Even rigidity can be handy at times.

There are certain experiences that I consider to be only on the borders of my personal therapy, but which have had a profound influence on the work I do as a Gestalt therapist. My experiences of painting models, of being visually "stoned," and of having my own body massaged have influenced the way I look at people.

I have always been visually curious. My visual curiosity carries enormous energy. I look people over and enjoy developing what I see into experiments and other learning experiences. Sometimes I touch people when I do body work, and my touching is based on what I have learned about my own body and how it works in various situations. I used to get a massage every week. Each time I would pay attention to how I deflected my awareness from sensation. For instance, I would suddenly lose an arm--I wouldn't remember when Al worked on it and it bothered me that I lost a whole tactual experience. I began to attend to every moment of being touched, where. I was touched, and the quality of the touch--whether it was rough, gentle, or stimulating, pressing against soft or dull parts of me, or pressing against my resistance. I learned a lot from that. When I touch someone, I touch respectfully.

It is impossible to work with a person without noticing the attitude of his/her body. The body not only expresses the person's present mood; it also speaks the secrets which are not yet carried in awareness. The body is the person's "truth button." It sings out beyond the person's words like a Greek chorus. There are times when I experiment with not listening to the words; I respond only to the singing out, the calling forth of the person's physical presence.

Another area of exposure which is of significance in my thinking is that of work. I find it important that a person be exposed to the greatest variety of work, from hard labor and simple concrete tasks, to complex problem-solving situations. However, I do not believe that suffering as such, or the stress and pain of survival, are necessary requirements for developing a full personal life.

In *The Prophet*, Kahlil Gibran (1960) spoke thus of work: "Always you have been told that work is a curse and labor a misfortune. But I say to you that when you work you fulfill a part of earth's furthest dream assigned to you when the dream was born. And in keeping yourself with labor you are in truth loving lives. And to love life through labor is to be intimate with life's inmost secrets..."

The greater the experiential space within the therapist, both horizontal and vertical, the more receptive s/he can be to the experience of the other. It is difficult to be a guide for someone on a journey without having some experience of the lay of the land, the topography of the surroundings.

There are some matters about a person that are not easily objectified. They may refer to his "spirit" or his/her sense of presence. A person may push others to do things, may be bent on performance, or may affect others without saying a word. S/he evokes feelings in other people simply because s/he is that person. This special evocative quality is cultivated in the person's character and becomes embedded in every sinew of his/her body.

I never worked through my mourning, my sadness. No matter how much I cry, my sense of mourning remains in the background. Yet, there is something inside me that feels indestructible. I have been pummeled so much that, in a sense, I have been tenderized. My suffering has softened me.

The fact that I am going to die is ever-present, and so is my sense of constant change. I am also in contact with a kind of grand plan and a grand humor about our lives. We are farts in the wind. This business of being a therapist, being accomplished, learning and getting a degree, having a family, is only a very tiny piece of the grand plan. My life experiences have given me a sense of humor and of tragedy about being here. It is a damn shame to die, having done so much building.

While I was in therapy, Erv sat in silence with me. He wasn't only waiting for me to produce; he was living through a process of mourning with me. When I finally broke through, I was able to weep. And ever since then I have been able to cry freely when I feel saddened.

Many of my colleagues will argue that one does not have to have experienced a great personal misfortune to help someone with a profound loss or with a terminal illness. I even agree with such statements. Yet, there is a difference between helping someone in such a journey and being prepared to fully participate in it in a way which is inspiring and moving for another person. It is one thing to help someone adjust to a situation. It is another to be a moving presence, a presence that stimulates spiritual ascendance rather than mere survival.

Rainer Maria Rilke (1949) spoke eloquently of the depth of preparation in the life of an artist:

> I think I ought to begin to do some work, now that I am learning to see. I am twenty-eight years old, and almost nothing has been done...Ah! But verses amount to so little when one writes them young. One ought to wait and gather sense and sweetness a whole life long, and a long life if possible, and then, quite at the end, one might perhaps be able to write ten lines that were good. For verses are not, as people imagine, simple feelings (those one has early enough)--they are experiences. For the sake of a single verse, one must see many cities, men and things, one must know the animals, one must feel how the birds fly and know the gesture with which the little flowers open in the morning. One must be able to think back to roads in unknown regions, to unexpected meetings and to partings one had long seen coming; to days of childhood that are still unexplained, to parents whom one had to hurt when they brought one some joy and one did not grasp it (it was

> a joy for someone else;) to childhood illnesses that so strangely begin with such a number of profound and grave transformations, to days in rooms withdrawn and quiet and to mornings by the sea, to the sea itself, to seas, to nights of travel that rushed along on high and flew with all the stars--and it is not yet enough if one may think of all this. One must have memories of many nights of love, none of which was like the others, of the screams of women in labor, and of light, white, sleeping women in childbed, closing again. But one must also have sat beside the dying, must have sat beside the dead in the room with the open window and the fitful noises. And still it is not enough to have memories. One must be able to forget them when they are many and one must have the great patience to wait until they come again. For it is not yet the memories themselves. Not till they have turned to blood within us, to glance and gesture, nameless and no longer to be distinguished from ourselves--not till then can it happen that in a most rare hour the first work of a verse arises in their midst and goes forth from them.

So I continue becoming a Person. It is only out of growing awareness of the humanness in me that one can receive or enhance the humanness in others. Without this developing knowledge, this schema of previous experience, the other person's articulated content will not penetrate one at the center--where it counts.

After having acquired all the theoretical and methodological awareness of the Gestalt process, one still has oneself to contend with. No amount of enriched content will inspire the impoverished soul. It is the person, the person alone, who is responsible for the aesthetic quality and affective depth of the creative process. Such is the artist's responsibility--and courage.

References

Gibran, K. (1960). *The Prophet*. New York, NY: Alfred Knopf.

Kopp, S. (1971). *Metaphors from a Therapist Guru.* Palo Alto, CA: Science and Behavior Books.

Rilke, R. (1949). *The notebooks of Malte Laurids Brigge.* M.D.H. Norton (Trans.). New York, NY: W.W. Norton.

Brooklyn, 1950

You fill me with a kaleidoscope of liveliness
Open me up and pour the world in -
Make me overflow into the world:
Contactful sponginess
Hallucinations of the world-starting-all-over-again
With its purity, brilliance
Yet twirling around as in coitus or birth labor:
Going in and out of focus
Hallucinations of world-coming-to-an-end:
Heart torn out of me
Yet all is well: Better than ever
Permeability will never kill me, it will purify and
Cleanse… tears cleanse
She-God-is-totally-loving
And never impatient
And her love sifts through me
Warming all the world

J.Z., 1969

I give to you with soul, guts
ask no questions, make no requests
Nothing matters but the act of moving toward
you
Flowers in hand.
Floating over the hamlets at
daybreak
I feel a thrust within ----
it says,
give all, give all!
Lovely
Exhilarating ----
I move toward you, my being touches
you with its gift ---
You move
ever-so-slowly gracefully in
response to me,
almost floating in slow-motion-
picture-fashion
we mingle in the act of giving
and taking
No witness could tell who gave and
who received.

J.Z., 1970

2

Searching for Clarity

Summer 1983

Jean Valjean

As a child in Poland, I saw a film in which the hero is unjustly imprisoned. It was probably based on Victor Hugo's Les Miserables. The image has stayed with me. The man, sweating and filthy, breaks out of his cell using his bare hands, he frees himself against all odds so that later he may free others. The image of "breaking out against all odds" was a metaphor for my early struggles as a child living in wartime Europe.

Although I had little understanding of life, and almost no formal education until I was seventeen, I had learned in the spaces of my body about hate, injustice, pain, fright… and also of the surprising freshness of the rising sun the morning after a bombing in some little town.

At one point, I was buried by a bomb blast. I did not speak or hear for many days. Being alive was a miracle. And sadness was, and remains, the ground of my life. The struggle of life against death, goodness against evil, remained themes in my life.

I came to America, a survivor of the holocaust. As is typical of my people--at least of pre-Israel days--I responded to my traumatic experiences with more grief than anger, more sadness than righteous indignation, more mourning than vengefulness. In short, I was a very sad seventeen-year-old who suffered nightly nightmares of Nazis chasing me while my legs became heavier and my body immobilized.

During my physical exam for induction to the U.S. Army, a prospect which made me feel hopeless, the physician found me extremely thin and pale, and looked for signs of addiction to drugs. I was interviewed by a young psychiatrist and told him about my nightmares. I was disqualified on the psychological grounds that I could not tolerate living through another war.

My life as a therapist began with a search for myself. In the beginning this search was characterized by an insatiable curiosity about language (I learned English at seventeen), art, electronics, philosophy, the images and appearances of the physical world. Mostly I was not able to learn well through reading. I learned by listening, looking, talking. I was grateful to be in America, to be allowed to work and to study.

My earliest and most powerful searchings were in the world of art. We lived in a railroad flat in Brooklyn. This meant that light traveled uninterrupted from one room to the next. I painted in the bathroom so I would not disturb anyone late at night. I spent many nights copying Van Gogh's self-portraits. His intensity was electric. I understood his love of the poor, his compassion for a prostitute, his passion for life, his guilt.

I remember an art assignment in high school in which we all made masks. My mask was different from the others, so much so that my own imagery frightened me. While the other students turned out more or less primitive facsimiles of human faces, my mask was more detailed and, at the same time, more disfigured. The man's face had one staring eye, while the other eye was hollow, oozing blood. His head was smashed in. I still have this mask, and I still gaze at it to remember how deeply pained I was. My internal life was a nightmare.

I am not quite sure how all this related to my early work as a therapist. I do know that even at that time I knew the propellant force of my pain, my nightmares, my fear of death. I knew inside myself that pain can become a force of transforming a life. It was not articulated that clearly inside of me. I knew the dangers of becoming infatuated with my suffering and making a profession of it. I knew that the only good about being a survivor was that a survivor must justify his life. A survivor has no right to dilly-dally with his life.

Pain turned me upon myself. It forced me to ask questions, to search. Pain turned me to meanings--to making sense of life as it is. I knew about pain, but I still didn't know how to enter into a relationship with someone else in pain. Pain--especially in a person not fully formed--makes it almost impossible to be invested in the care of others.

Not having been indoctrinated by my parents' Judaic beliefs during the war years, I found myself turning cold to holy prayer days in which we asked God for forgiveness, prayed for his mercy and protection against enemies who might wish to harm us.

The whole procedure seemed ludicrous and confusing. What were my sins? How had God protected most of my family who were wiped out? And if he took special care to look out for me, what rhyme or reason was there in this act? After all, there were many thousands of people who were making enormous contributions to humanity: writers, scientists, rabbis--people who had given their lives in the service of others. For what? What were their unforgivable sins? Perhaps, I said to myself, this God was kinder to previous generations of Jews in exile from Jerusalem for 2,000 years, but he was no friend of mine.

So as not to displease my parents, I continued attending high holy day services, but while no one looked I read Freud and Karen Horney's *Self Analysis*.

Sartre

In college I gave up all ideas of some absolutism outside myself. God was an Indian-giver. What good was it to be of the chosen people and then to be slaughtered senselessly? There was nothing and no one all good up there--or all bad. All liturgy became mechanical and meaningless to me. The post-war existentialism of Sartre, Frankl, and others stimulated me to reread the old testament, substituting "I" for "God," for example, "In the beginning I created…" etc. There was no intrinsic meaning in my life, and looking for a preformed, ideal meaning was absurd. I created my own life, my own meanings. I was born alone, and I would die alone. No one else could make my life. I was responsible for my behavior, good and bad.

I read T.S. Eliot, James Joyce, and I stared at Picasso's "Guernica" and the works of other modern painters. There was no promise of clarity (the sort one sees in a Shakespeare, a Durer, Rubin, or Bach), but there was intense beauty in the organized fragmentation of the world portrayed by these contemporary artists. This was more like my life.

I loved the immediacy of experience. Existential analysis promised finding meaning in my own life. Painting and opera taught me the appreciation of process, of work going through stages, of its energizing possibilities and its culminating power. I find myself mentioning the arts over and over again and now a theme begins to grow: the theme of therapy as an art form.

Perls

Fritz Perls couldn't stand my sadness, self-deprecation and my requests for more lectures from him. I awakened as if from a dream that I was bowing down to people with whom I acted like a coolie. He taught me not to diminish myself with my unaware niceness. He and Erv Polster helped me to contact my own rage, my own "Nazism," and to express it. What good was my niceness without my meanness, or my truthfulness without my lying? The notion of polarities became very important, and that these polarities could be discovered in oneself by simply staying with present experience, letting the experience grow, letting it become as large as it wishes, and letting the experience become "fulfilled"--to have its own natural culmination.

There is no way of letting this process develop--"to have its way"--without expressing myself, acting. Transformation is a process starting with simple, superficial awareness which energizes us to movement. One way to become transformed is to act, to move one's body, to be expressive, alive. I learned that awareness cannot remain vital inside of us, that its full vitality is asserted in activity and, later, a sense of completion.

I later realized that this was what the existential analysts hinted at--only half aware--when they praised the understanding of one's "isness," one's simply being. I learned from my Gestalt colleagues that isness is a process, a dance, a never-ending movement, and not simply cortical awareness of self.

And so, in the 1960s, I became fascinated with entering a person's existence through the vehicle of movement, rather than through awareness alone. I realized that, in the cycle of behavior, movement stimulates fresh awareness and that new awarenesses generate novel movements. All this I wrote about under titles like "Dream Work as Theatre" and "Individual and Group Experiment." I didn't need to explain myself to people in workshops, finding explanations cumbersome. Besides, it was a real high to be a young guru who taught by doing. My being was coming to life. For the first time in my life I didn't need to justify my methods, as long as they yielded dramatic results.

Slowly, I began to sense a metamorphosis in my body, a gradual change from a depressed, hunched-over, mourning, "old" refugee to a young man discovering love, dance, and the meaning of celebration.

I didn't know that people responded to me not simply because I was charismatic or energetic or smart. I realized later that my clients were wiser than I because they must have responded also to my giving without giving myself away. In later years I learned that my grounded presence was helpful to people, that people cared more about what is evoked inside themselves than about being shocked into change through provocative anxiety arousal.

In my late twenties, I started shifting from mourning to optimism. My doctoral dissertation integrated the concept of death with personality growth. I discovered that a poor black woman could "grow" (in Maslowian terms) while dying of cancer. In another paper, I explored two personality patterns in dying patients: those who would "cling" and those who would "let go." Looking back, I realize that in my own existence I was no longer clinging to my fear of dying, that I was too busy living my life to worry about death. Having completed my doctorate, I dropped the study of dying in 1963, shifting to the study of living as a creative venture.

Thirteen years later I wrote Creative Process in Gestalt Therapy, as an effort to integrate the emphasis on spontaneous experimentation with theory, meaning, and structure. I was stimulated to speak to the question of therapy as an art form. I found that not only does any given experience have movement, form, and natural grace, but that the therapeutic hour itself can have integrity, wholeness, and beauty.

And so, all my love of painting, theatre, music, came full circle and became integrated with my work as a therapist. Only the medium had changed. The medium of a human life is grander, more frightening, dangerous, more plastic, dynamic, and complex. A painting can't refuse to change--one only needs to deal with one's own internal resistances--but person's can say “No!” and their “no” is part of their dignity, integrity, and struggle to learn actively and responsibly rather than swallowing what a therapist may be force-feeding them.

The Nature of Change

I seem to be learning over and over again that people can change when I can help them lean fully into what they already are, that only when a “stingy” person can embrace his or her stinginess fully and with pleasure, is there any hope that he or she can flow into generosity. The paradox is that when you are permitted to do the forbidden, unacceptable thing fully, you then become naturally aroused by other options, other possibilities. When someone asks me to attend to how I am sitting, I become interested in my caved-in chest. If I keep staying with that collapsed state, I will spontaneously experiment with sitting differently. On the other hand, if I am told that I am slouching and to try “sitting up straight,” I feel my resistance growing even as I try to please the other person.

Systems

Existentialism, the spirit of the sixties, and my own focusing on myself, reinforced my work with individuals. A married man with two pretty daughters and a number of friends, I was alone. Looking back, I remember how I was painfully shy in graduate school, how I was willing to write two papers instead of one rather than giving a presentation to a classroom of peers. My profession as a therapist gave a supportive structure to practice being intimate with others in a more or less safe atmosphere. I was generous and warm to my patients and students, and they reciprocated.

As the years passed, and my marriage to Florence survived many crises, I became interested in intimacy and in the tenaciousness of people moving toward each other. I became more actively interested in my fathering and in how my children "daughtered" me. Later, it became evident to me (in my gut, not just my brain) that a family or group is not a simple conglomerate of self-supporting persons, but a gestalt, a system which is greater than the sum of its members.

I became aware--with inspiration from my friend, Sonia Nevis--that, for example, I didn't project alone: that in order for me to project on Florence, also an example, she would have to be willing to swallow or stay silent, or not be willing to correct me and vice versa--that projections, introjections, retroflections, deflections are systems phenomena--that we all cooperate to make something unsatisfactory, unfinished, or to make it complete and good.

System thinking has also influenced my work with groups. I have learned that people need to be reminded of their competence, that if I can manage to follow and later articulate the process of the group, people will use the process well.

Once again I find that I don't have to make something happen, that activity can be tapped from the group's own energy pool with my presence, groundedness, and a full interest in the phenomena of interactions between members. When given adequate support and clear structure, people surprise themselves with the variety and depth of their giving and taking.

Therapist As Teacher

As I approach fifty, I find myself enjoying more of my teaching role with my clients: slowing people down, helping them to chew, to listen, and to see. And I am particularly savoring my client's requests that tap into this teaching skill.

There are no absolutes after all. Life and therapy are the same process of staying and struggling with oneself and with each other, and resolving the unfinished--only to discover at that very moment that one has started with another dilemma that awaits completion.

The puzzlement of lacking clarity energizes us to move on until death saves us all from the final restfulness.

I experience less and less limitations of categorical thinking, "principle thinking" about the world and its people. I feel more measured and respectful of the complexity, the problematic and paradoxical nature of our lives.

I have a clearer sense of the meaning of compassion and generosity in relationships. If a husband and wife are fighting, I can appreciate the validity of each one's experience. If I am generous, I can tell each how I understand their way of seeing reality.

That reminds me of a story of a rabbi in Poland who received a couple for counseling.

"Reb Chaim," pleaded the husband, "I study the Torah all day and Rivka keeps interrupting me all the time..."

"I understand how disturbing that must be, Jacob," the rabbi responded.

Then Rivka spoke: "Rabbi, this husband of mine has not brought one groshe home to buy challa for the Sabbath. I am tearing my hair out in despair!"

"I can see how frustrating it must be to see Jacob study and not bring any money home. You must be a very patient woman," said Reb Chaim.

While all this was going on, the rabbi's good wife, Shulamit, was listening. Shulamit decided to help her husband: "Chaim, you are telling the husband that he is right, and you are telling the wife that she is also right. Doesn't that make it hard to make a judgment?"

Reb Chaim looked warmly at his wife, stroked his beard thoughtfully, and responded softly, "I see what you mean, Shulamit, and you are right, too."

My perception of myself and of human interactions is more compassionate and I appreciate increasingly the aesthetic richness of life around me. My sense of the aesthetic seems fuller, broader, and is interwoven with humor and a sense of the philosophical.

At this moment, I can't tell if I truly feel this way, or whether I am simply outlining my next struggle for clarity.

All day I have bathed in deeply stirred
souls,
My eyes glowing, my body moving with the
spring winds,
And now, at midnight, I rest in the lines
of your body,
My soul sinking into nothingness.

We spoke well, my dear love and
We touched each other with wisdom
born of the moment
But now the snow has fallen and all
is silent.

J.Z.,1969

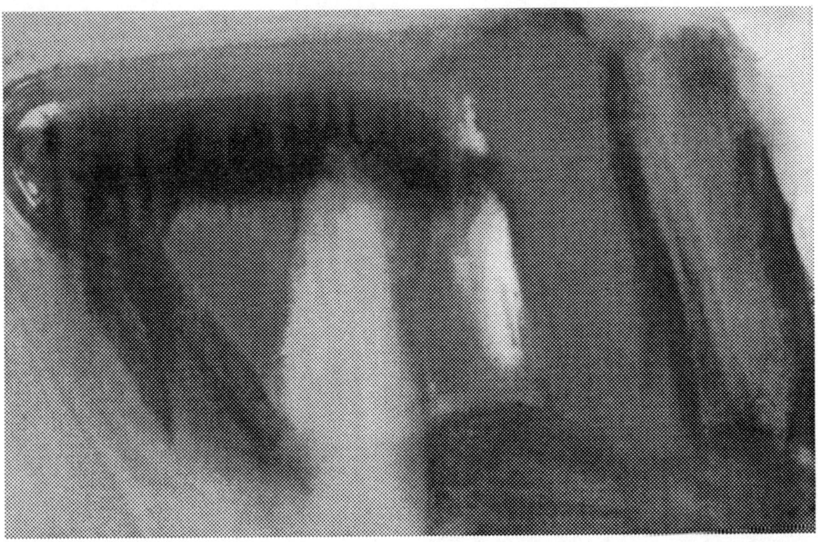

1980

3

The Therapist As Artist

1974

I. Integrity and Change

Psychotherapy is a lively process. The process involves stoking one's inner fires of awareness and contact; it involves exchanges of energy with the other--exchanges which stimulate and nourish the other but do not deplete one's own vitality and power.

The patient has personal integrity. This means that he has developed, over a span of many years, modes of moving in the world which have structural and functional unity for him. This unity also includes his "symptoms" and complaints and behaviors which, in the therapist's view, hamper the patient's capacity to change. This whole bundle of feelings, physical stances, and verbal styles comprise the person's "integrity" and he comes to a group or into individual therapy not so much to change this sense of being himself as to exercise it.

Creative process in psychotherapy has basically two elements: one is for the therapist to be on friendly terms with this personal integrity presented to him; to use one's whole being in a full study of "what it is like to be a person like this"--to bend one's shoulders, to tighten one's ass, just to get into that sort of posture of being in the world. This is a kind of loving curiosity, a lively state of naturalistically learning the other's life space.

The second element in the creative process is revolutionary molding. Here the therapist identifies with the most radical aspects of his patient's personality, the part of his personality that is often waiting for permission to experiment with novel or truly startling ways of experiencing himself.

The patient is always in the existential dilemma of being torn between the painful comfort of his existing integrity and his need to change. Generally, creative process is hampered when patient and therapist unwittingly identify with the separate parts of the patient's personality. The therapist begs for change and the patient fights for his "integrity." In this collusion, the revolutionary in the patient is projected to the therapist and the patient then conveniently "fights" with his own projection.

In the creative process, the therapist enables the patient to join with him in an adventure in which the pair can constantly play both parts of this conflict drama. The therapist helps the other to be the experimenter, the teacher, the active modifier, while he floats in the caring attitude of understanding and respecting the patient's existing "integrity." It is in this process of rhythmic sharing and active exploration of a person's inner life that his original personal structure, his integrity, begins to change.

II. The Phenomenological Base

In my work I always begin with what is there for the person (or the group) rather than with some arbitrary notion of what should be there (Zinker, 1972). I try to understand and to feel--and to psychologically gargle--the other's mode of being in the world. Like a sculptor getting in contact with the odor, shape, and grain of the wood he carves, I try to stay with the configurations of the other person's experience. But even though I respect the validity of his experience, and his way of seeing the feeling, I am driving to expose him to a new way, a new visual or cognitive or motoric perspective of himself. This new perspective or dimension does not have to be cataclysmically dramatic; it needs merely to respectfully move the existing system into a slightly fresher view of itself. For example, a woman says that she feels childlike. Upon questioning, she explains some of the ways in which she knows about her childlike nature. I then ask her to act out her childlike behavior with me or with the group. The reason I ask her to do this is that, generally, she only has a conceptual notion of what "childlike" means, and she needs a more expansive view of all that "childlike" implies for her. I also ask her to do something that is anchored in her own experience, to her view of herself right now. Now, the implication and possible meanings and outcomes of such a simple experiment are enormous. They involve exaggeration of one polarity of self, observations related to posture (how she carries herself as a child, for example), language, voice quality, support systems of various types, and the therapist's silent, theoretical, clinical formulations about, let's say, the undeveloped adult behavior or experience in this particular person. So this little experiment is only the beginning of work--a mere behavioral extension of the words presented to the therapist at that moment. Most importantly, the experiment offers:

To expand the person's repertoire of behavior.

To create conditions under which the person can see his life as his own creation. (Ownership of therapy).

To stimulate the person's experiential learning and the evolution of new self concepts from behavioral creations.

To complete unfinished situations and to overcome blockages in the awareness-contact cycle.

To integrate cortical understandings with motoric discoveries.

To discover polarizations which are not in awareness.

To stimulate the integration of conflictual forces in the personality (In this case, "child woman" vs. "adult woman.")

To dislodge and reintegrate introjects and to generally place "misplaced" feelings, ideas and actions where they belong in the personality.

To stimulate circumstances under which the person can feel and act stronger, more competent, more self supported, more explorative and actively responsible for himself.

I start with the surface acceptance of this person's experience of her "child." It is a given. I don't try to persuade her that it isn't so; rather, as the work develops and she feels a sense of readiness, we can move into more difficult aspects of her self--parts which were originally difficult to bring into awareness and to share with others.

III. Emphasis on Process

I go up to my studio to paint. I get up there and realize I don't feel like painting. So I putter around. I clean brushes, or prime canvases, or look at pictures in magazines. I do the things that are possible for me at that moment and I allow myself room to build my imagery and excitement until I become ready to make something. It may only be a paper cutout, but it is just what I am ready to do at this point in my creative process (Baron, 1969; Koestler, 1964).

And so it is with me as a therapist. One cannot "push the river" and make art. The patient must be taken through a graded series of experiences before he is ready to grasp a new notion about himself and to behaviorally move in that direction. You can order someone around to do things for you, and the patient may even cooperate, but if the process of building readiness is not there for the other, nothing significant happens, other than perhaps getting into an argument, or feeling flat, or feeling that we are not, somchow, communicating with each other. Much of therapy consists of stoking the fire, nurturing a particular theme, building support in areas of verbalization or action where support is needed--it is like priming the canvas and cleaning the brushes.

Another part of the process in psychotherapy is the notion of staying open to a myriad of possibilities for the person or the group. Every new hypothesis or actual exchange or experiment should be considered an exploration, a possibility--which, if it "catches fire" for the person, will be taken further and further to the deepest layers of the personality.

Although I may have two or three possibilities for outcomes somewhere out there, I cannot squeeze these outcomes from a patient. I must be willing to count every shrub and pebble on the road before I get to the color and excitement of the city at the end of it. When the person reaches the insight or resolution at the end of such a respectful process journey, the insight and the satisfaction are full and whole and obvious to him and to his group and to his therapist. It takes time to be born. It takes patience to be a good midwife.

IV. Creation As Problem Solving: Diagnostic Formulations, Clinical Hunches, Cognitive Maps

The therapist-creator is not a decerebrate fish! He is not just a feeler and empathizer. It is sheer foolishness to throw out "labels" just because it is not fashionable to be intellectual, to be a "mind-fucker." It is fine to use your mind as long as it has intercourse with the rest of your being and not just with itself alone. I need to know what is "going on" with my group or my patient at the least, I need to have some formulations about what goes on. It is far better to travel to the city with some sort of map (and to know many alternative routes) than to get lost in a hundred blind alleys and feel helpless or get angry out of frustration.

Every therapeutic encounter is a search for, and partial resolution of a "problem" in the broadest aesthetic meaning of that term. If I start with a blank canvas and I make a red, round mass in the middle of this canvas--and if I want to make a painting beyond that initial mass of color--then I have a problem to solve. Where do I go next? What color next? What shape? How to balance? Or to work on asymmetry and make the asymmetry "work" for the painting? So it is with therapy, but a thousand times more complex.

I want to share a particular case with you: Ron, an engineer in one of my groups in Florida, wants to "work" with me in the group. He is thin, delicate, his movements are very feminine. In my head I think about these things before he opens his mouth to offer a dream. (I experience the dream in this case as a delaying action--the telling of it has no apparent energy for this man.) I wait for him to say more; why jump on a lifeless dream? I think about homosexuality, about the mother who flatters and tries to control and swallow her son--and the father who is either absent, reflective, crude, or angry in the rocking chair while mother does her thing to the son. At the same time I am looking at the man before me. He is, in my estimate, a beautiful man. I like him. I have a fantasy of myself as his father. How I would love him and have fun with him if I were his father. I continue staying with him in the process without sharing most of these thoughts and fantasies. I listen and I take him in feeling-fully. I am feeling rich and full inside during this whole thing. I ask him:

Joseph: Where is your energy now?

Ron: In my face - it's hot and burning. I am afraid of what the people will think of me, of making a fool of myself.

Joseph: You sound like you fear 'losing face.'

Ron: Yes, I do.

All these previous thoughts are temporarily filed away perhaps for later use. In the meantime, I am working with Ron's face. I offer a temporary solution for the "losing face" problem; I think to myself, he always looks so serious and his face is so controlled, distant and mask-like. I suggest an experiment.

Joseph: Could you 'lean into' losing face and do it literally by 'giving up' your face and making faces at people?

He agrees to this. Once he lets go a bit, he is masterful at making faces--especially at thc women. After making faces some more, he reports, "I feel better, more relaxed, not as afraid of what people will think..."

This is a very long session, and I will not go into all of it here, but later on he tells the group about his mother and how he is so angry with her and so scared of her, and to this day he does not look fully into her face. Now, my formulations about this man are coming into focus, and I continue working with his face and the notion of taking women in through his face. He tries to take one of the women in through his eyes and partially succeeds and feels wonderful about his efforts.

All through this process, diagnostic labels are not mentioned and dynamic/analytic thoughts are not discussed, but rather "sifted through" the patient's actual experience and transformed into behavioral experiments. The larger problem worked on has to do (in part) with the patient's relationships with women. And I feel so pleased that I have "cognitive handles" inside of me throughout the process. Some of them were extremely helpful, indeed, while others were discarded (Gordon, 1971; Polster & Polster, 1973).

V. The Creative Leap

The beauty of Gestalt therapy for me is that it allows me to be phenomenologically true to what is there and, at the same time, allows me to translate my own creative hunches into experimental acts. At best, these acts have the possibility of breaking through existing character patterns, and, at worst, they don't work or they backfire. One must have a good feeling for (and with) the patient and/or the group, to jump the gun and ask them to do or think something brand new. And one should have some sense of "good taste," or perhaps one might call it the sense of the acceptable aesthetic in the particular system within which one finds oneself. Asking the person a coarse or ugly question, or an insensitive one, may not only be "tasteless," but puts one in a position of bullying, bulldozing, and insulting the other; and then one must deal with unnecessary conflicts of one's own making.

The creative leap comes out of a combination of one's clinical hunches and one's outrageous inventiveness. In the case of Ron, above, I said to him at one point, "Tell me about your hate for your mother." Although I had a sense inside of me that he "had to" have difficulty with this woman, nowhere in the previous work had we discussed this, nor did I prepare him for it. I was ready to be told that I was full of beans, but I was also ready to respond to Ron's increased feeling and his sharing of how he had to close off his anger with her by stiffening his face toward her and, indeed, toward everyone else. What a chance to take! I was really frightened and excited at the same time as I allowed these words to slip out of me. This time it worked in the right direction and, as a result, we moved into a series of experiments that became extremely important revelations to Ron. One experiment of looking at a woman and trying to take her through the eyes and mouth was a behavioral extension of this initial thrust of new energy in Ron. This experiment was a creative leap from merely discussing his mother to active work with a living, breathing woman in the group. This kind of leaping--of jumping over possible objections or resistances--is the defining characteristic of the creative process in all areas of living and working, not just in Gestalt therapy. To do it well, one must take chances of momentarily failing, shifting gears and moving on to something else that seems to work better or shifting to that which the patient finds more palatable and ego-syntonic.

The creative leap breaks the rules of constantly staying with the process. Innovation often calls for the breaking of rules. One must, after all, attend to and respect one's own inventiveness and intellectual "jumps" and one's own capacity to shape the ongoing action. It is this aspect of psychotherapy that keeps me most enlivened.

Creative process has a balance between the phenomenological base of what is there on the one hand and behavioral jumping into strange territories on the other.

VI. Context and Metaphor

A man says he has a problem with his kids, so I think of him as a teacher, or a baby-sitter, or an animal with a litter.

I think of him as a kid--maybe I should have him behave as if he is the troublesome kid described--and see what happens, because I already know that his context, his metaphor, his literal way, his non-playful approach does not work. That is why he is here asking for help.

So he plays the kid that keeps doing "bad" things to attract attention. Then he says, "Dad, I want you to take me with you on your next trip." He realizes that he has not heard his son before (one level), and is neglecting the inner voice of his own child on another level. The new metaphor invented in my head turns out more helpful than I originally expected because, you see, I never had an answer for him, I just played with a new way of experiencing that particular dilemma. There is no magic in it--just a kind of emotively intellectual boldness that puts the data on a different conceptual channel.

He is telling me a very serious story and his face is a mask--or his voice is whiny or he is hunched over, or he is not breathing, or he is sweating like hell in an air conditioned room and so on and on. And as long as I can be there, listening to my own songs, seeing my own hallucinations, inventing my own peculiar humor without falling into his limited view of the situation, then I stay alive and he has a chance of coming to life, by moving into a new channel in himself, by seeing himself in a brand new mirror (Gordon, 1971). One must be free from attachment to the patient's perspective or the material he produces the way Ram Dass is free from his "thinking" and "sensing" in order that his awareness can become like a laser beam (Ram Dass, 1974). Also, in order to make new metaphors, one must be free from attachment to one's own needs, needs that limit one's intellectual scope, needs for success or approval or sexual satisfaction.

In order to invent new contexts for the other person, I must learn how to listen to him without wanting, to touch without desiring, to love without squeezing, to gaze without becoming overly pedantic. It is this sort of inner space, inner freedom, which enhances the creation of yet unexplored experiential channels for my patient, for myself, and for both of us as we encounter each other (Gordon, 1971; Ram Dass, 1974).

In short, the process of Gestalt psychotherapy is not only the continuous invention of new models of seeing oneself. It is also a continuous behavioral testing of these novel models in the safety of a creatively permissive environment.

VII. Sense of Power and Magic

A wise man once told me that what is taken as psychotherapeutic magic by the innocent witness is only the outcome of many years of struggling and learning on the part of the experienced therapist. The concert pianist practices five hours a day for a lifetime. He makes awful mistakes. He struggles with his conscience, his values. He is purified by his suffering, his self-criticism, and by interspersed successful outcomes that come in tiny little dosages. Then he performs on the stage and people say that God is in his hands, that he makes miracles. The fact is that the creative person, the creative therapist, is a disciplined craftsman whose gift is to keep reaching out toward his most profound personal potential. It is this practicing with love and reaching beyond himself without stereotypic and shallow self seeking and righteousness that has the makings for a creative person. I don't mean to sound glib, puritanical, or evangelistic. The reality for me is that deep down I am a pleasure seeker and that making something new with other people and in our mutual lives gives me great pleasure and enormous joy. It is during this process of transcending my own heaviness or dullness or sterotypy that I feel pure, good, beautiful, powerful, holy, rich, sweet, magical. This feeling, when it is there, is not only my own--it saturates the space around me and is exuded by the other person or persons who share it. And it is not clear if God is in our hands and hearts, whether we are in his lap, or if this is the way artists create God. Perhaps it does not matter. At those rare moments of creativeness, when an ordinary person has something in common with the making of the universe, he feels a sense of transcendence, of moving beyond his daily life (Castaneda, 1968; Koestler, 1964; Maslow, 1971). What can be a greater reward?

VIII. Generating and Transforming Energy Systems

In order for a person to "work" in therapy and, consequently, to change, he needs energy. Generally he has enough energy to come to my office or to a weekend group, but that does not guarantee that he has energy to work on himself. Often his energy is locked in the muscular (or systemic) frozenness of his character structure, or, as most people like to see it, in his "resistances." Actually, there is no functional or structural difference between character frozenness and resistances. A resistance is what the therapist experiences. The patient is merely being the person he thinks himself to be and he experiences taking care of himself. So the person's energy and its focus may not be in his awareness (Zinker, 1972). It may be experienced in a negative way; i.e., being aware of stiffness in one's knees or, say, pain in one's chest.

The therapist's job is to locate, mobilize and modify this energy in the service of new, more adaptive, more fluid behavior.

In Ron's case, I didn't experience much energy in his dream. What he felt more urgently at the moment was the flush and tension in his face, and so it was this facial energy that yielded the most work and most of his behavioral change during the therapy hour. Often there is little energy in the person's verbalizations. They are only habit tapes that are well rehearsed and impenetrable. The therapist often falls into the trap of exchanging energy-depleting, sterile words with the patient, with the resulting sense of heaviness and even depression in both therapist and patient. (How often I still fall into this trap.) The patient does what is easiest for him, but the therapist can't afford this "luxury" simply because he becomes more and more removed from where the patient is perking, where the action really is in the arena of therapeutic change.

I am talking with Betty. She feels flat and immobilized. She feels she cannot survive in this competitive world. She goes on and on. I am beginning to feel drained. My energy depletion tells me that her energy system is frozen and that she is sucking it from me. At this point I stop listening to her words and watch her body. Her arms and legs look bloated and stiff at the same time. I bring her attention to her body. She says, "I feel tight in my legs and my arms." At this point I ask her to imagine what she could do with her stiff sensations--how she could use the muscles that are stiff. She has an image of running. I ask her to close her eyes and go back in her life and visualize running. The following story emerges: Betty is 10 years old. She is in camp and there is a running contest. Everyone in her tent believes that she will be the winner for her tent. She feels increasingly pressured and frightened of failure. The outcome is that she loses the contest for her tent. After the telling of the story, Betty gets in touch with her anger with the kids in camp for pressuring and pushing her. I ask her to see if she could use her arms and legs (where the energy is frozen) to express the anger on some large pillows. Betty is flying high at this point--she is ready to express her anger. The energy flows visibly within her. She kicks and punches the pillows repeatedly. She yells at the kids and her voice gains strength. She goes back to her chair breathing heavily: "I feel so loose and strong. I feel like I can go out there and do what I need to do for myself. I am not going to let people step on me." Betty's frozen energy has been freed up and mobilized in the service of adaptation, behavioral flow and a general sense of well-being.

My reward in this process is not only that I got her off her stuckness, but that I, myself, feel more enlivened and less drained.

If energy is nowhere to be located in the person, then it can be "pumped up." In one other actually very similar case, I asked the person to run in circles in my room. He said it was silly. So I offered to run with him. We ran together for what seemed like ten minutes. I fell back exhausted in my chair, but my patient was revivified and proceeded to work on a serious problem involving his sexuality. Apparently the running stimulated sexual sensations and sexual anxieties as well.

One needs "juice" to make creations, and if the juice is not in the person's feeling life or his language, then it is surely somewhere in his body. The recovery of body energy feeds the person's affect and puts color into the content of his language (Polster & Polster, 1973).

IX. Novel Integrations

Part of the creativity in Gestalt therapy is to integrate polarities in the patient's personality (Fantz, 1973). The person often identifies himself with one characteristic and not its counterpart i.e., he sees himself as peaceful and not aggressive, or stingy and not generous, or honest and not devious, and so on.

It is certainly easy to try to question these views of himself or to challenge him to stimulate his thinking in another direction. These verbal exchanges lay the cognitive ground for changes in the person's restrictive self-concept. But they need to be reinforced and driven home by experiments. The experiment does not only offer to exaggerate the person's polarized behavior; most importantly it makes for creative integration of his polarities and for greater wholeness of experience and expression.

After many months of therapy, Mrs. Miller, a professional singer, confesses to me that she has not been able to achieve an orgasm for the seven years of her marriage. I begin to fantasize about the orgiastic feelings she must get when she sings as a soloist with a large chorus and a full symphony orchestra. After a tentative inquiry, she volunteers to sing for me. And so, for a number of sessions, we work on her body awareness while she sings. In the process, she discovers enormously intense feelings in her abdomen and her vagina while singing. I then suggest that, as she sings for me, she close her eyes and visualize having intercourse with her husband. She feels embarrassed, so I volunteer to turn around. This makes the experiment more comfortable for her, and she proceeds. At the end of the session, she informs me, "I almost came while singing today and thinking about John." Several months later, she and her husband, John, came to a session with a bottle of wine to celebrate Sandra's first orgasmic experience during intercourse. It has been years since I have seen the Millers, and I sometimes wonder if she also gets orgasms when she sings. If so, I don't think it is a high price to pay for a more blissful sex life and wholesome marriage.

I want to tell you of another case of integration. The patient in this instance was a priest. He doesn't want to be called "Father," because it makes me feel impotent. It makes me feel like I have no balls." So I ask him to bless everyone in the group with his right hand, while he holds his crotch with his left! He begins to get into his potency. His blessings become more and more inspired and beautiful. With each person the blessing develops more sensitively, giving recognition of the other person's area of need. The priest becomes lively and there is more color in his face. The blessings are like spiritual explosions and, as he nears the last person, I notice that several people are weeping.

What seemed like a crude and vulgar experiment in the beginning, turned into a deeply insightful experience for this lovely man. As he finished the experiment there was a long silence in the group. He looked around, gazing warmly into our faces. "I think it would be nice if you called me 'Father' from time to time," he said.

He was able to integrate his sexual potency with his religious role as a "Father." This may seem very easy and simple, but for this priest it was one of the most powerful and integrating experiences of his life.

X. Creation As Tao Learning

Tao learning takes place in the total organism when the organism experiences its own force of movement and its own exploratory possibilities. Unlike deficit learning which takes place on a verbal-conceptual level, Tao learning is initiated by the person, and the person is allowed to move gracefully from one minute step in his process to his own next step. This step-by-step movement of imagery, muscular tension, verbalization and release gives the person a sense of ongoing creation of his destiny. He gradually begins to value his own process for its own sake as process, rather than bypassing the scenes on the way to a puzzlingly unclear goal - a goal which is often experienced as belonging to "them," to the other, to the parent or the therapist. It is extremely important that the person learn to value and enjoy his own fluidity within the trajectory of his work; and it is also important that he experience the therapist (or teacher) as his lubricant, rather than the source of his knowledge. Many months of valuable time are wasted when therapist and client collude to make the therapist the source of the knowledge and the client a child-cripple who needs to hear the wise man's answers.

It takes immaculate discipline on the part of the therapist (and joyful curiosity) to stay with the other's process without prematurely "pinching" it off with not yet fully formed statements of explanation or clarification. These premature moves generally come from the therapist's own anxiety to justify his role as helper and wise man; they don't come from respectful attending to the aesthetic nature of the other as moving through time and space in a valid pathway. The therapist, when he can lean into this sort of aesthetic appreciation, is a "naturalist"--a lover of "human nature."

Allowing the process to unfold does not mean giving up my potency, because I am always there pushing, prodding, enjoying, laughing, and also flowing in my sense of wonderment and fascination. This stance gives me the freedom to also be a learner, a student, and to make internal hypotheses rather than getting stuck with stale "eternal" truths pasted with routine self-righteousness upon every client.

XI. Impeccability

The creative therapist's biggest enemies are his desires to please and help, his exhibitionism, and dishonesty. All you need to do is walk down the streets of Greenwich Village or some summer resort and you will see thousands of paintings that are shallow attempts to please the eye and find the buyer. As a social being, the therapist/artist is always responding to his culture and to his friends. His challenge is to convert his need to please, or explain, or to be praised, into an internal energy system that feeds his uncompromising artistic standards. I call this stance "impeccability." Only the artist can judge, and knows deeply within himself, about his honesty. He knows when he is performing theater. He knows when he merely wants to make others laugh, or cry, or be impressed. The moment he loses touch with his honesty, at that moment he has lost his impeccable, uncompromising center. For example, as I write these words, I am sometimes enamored by the words themselves and how they sound to you, the reader. I suspect myself. One must always suspect oneself without making oneself sick (Castaneda, 1968). For example, I cannot really justify the above use of the word "center." It is an unnecessary word. It makes my writing more dramatic and perhaps romantically sentimental rather than truly accurate. I strive for impeccability, and purity of motives and process of the work itself.

Another way of referring to impeccability is to think of discipline. One must develop a method of work that has structure and continuity. One must trust one's process. One must be willing to be the master and to be the pupil in one body. One must be critical in a loving way rather than in a punitive way, because the artist only has himself, and he cannot bite the hand that makes him happy.

XII. Concluding Musings

Creativity is a celebration of one's grandeur, one's own sense of making anything possible. Creativity is a celebration of life--my celebration of my aliveness in the world. It is a bold statement of "I am here, I love me, I love life, I can be anything, I can do anything." Creativity is the practice of the presence of God in my hands, eyes, brain--in all of me. Creativeness is not merely the conception, but the act itself, the assertiveness of that which is urgent, which asks to be stated--to be shared.

Creative expression is a social act--a sharing with one's fellow man of this celebration, this assertion in living a full life. It is a statement of one's aesthetic appreciation.

It does not matter what field of endeavor we are talking about. In every field it is the same act of celebration, the same fullness of expression that justifies one's own purpose of living.

Finally, creativity is an "act of bravery." It states, "I am brave enough to do this thing at the possible cost of failure or ridicule, so that I may experience this day with newness and freshness."

References

Baron, F. (1969). *Creative person and creative process.* New York, NY: Holt, Rinehart & Winston.

Castaneda, C. (1968). *The teachings of Don Juan.* New York, NY: Ballantine.

Fantz, R. (1973). Polarities: Differentiation and integration. Cleveland, OH: Gestalt Institute of Cleveland.

Gordon, W. (1971). *Synectics.* New York, NY: Collier Books.

Herrigel, E. (1971). *Zen and the art of archery.* New York, NY: Vintage Books.

Koestler, A. (1964). *The act of creation.* New York, NY: Dell Books.

Maslow, A. (1971). *The farther reaches of human nature.* New York,

NY: Viking Press.
Polster, E., & Polster, M. (1973). *Gestalt therapy integrated.* New York, NY: Brunner/Mazel.
Ram Dass, B. (1974). *The only dance there is.* New York: Anchor Books/Doubleday Co.
Zinker, J., & Hallenbeck, C. (1962). Notes on loss, crisis and growth. Paper presented at Gestalt Institute of Cleveland, Cleveland, OH, November 4.
Zinker, J. (1968). On public knowledge and personal revelation, *Explorations*, October 15.
Zinker, J. (1971a). On loving encounters: A phenomenological view. Cleveland, OH: Gestalt Institute of Cleveland.
Zinker, J. (1971b). Dreamwork as theater, *Voices, 7*(2).
Zinker, J. (1972). The phenomenological here and now. Cleveland, OH: Gestalt Institute of Cleveland.
Zinker, J. (1974). Gestalt therapy is permission to be creative," *Voices, 9*(4).

April Dream

Last night my house was burning. Could not find
one precious thing to grab and find comfort in.
And when the torrential rain hammered out the
flames, I was angry with its self-righteous
interference.

My house is still burning. And where it is
whole, I have not found all the rooms,
closets and old garbage. There is no longer
a complacent order. Havoc has its own
integrity. Charred walls accept young vines
and holes in roof allow the fragrant spring
to freely visit.

My house is not my castle. It is not the
precious final coagulated fulfillment of
ironed-out dreams. It is a plant, a tree
swaying in the evening wind.

J.Z., 1970

1976

4

Presence as Evocative Power in Therapy

Summer 1987

Presence

To evoke is to send a message from something intrinsic in oneself that does not intend to move another. I may evoke something in you when I sit with you in silence without making a formal intervention. Evocative power is expressed in being fully present, fully there with a patient or a client system.

To provoke is to get a reaction because you are consciously pushing for one--you may be interrogating, questioning, pointing out, pointing to something in particular, or "setting up" a situation.

Psychotherapy requires a balance of evocative and provocative interventions on the part of the therapist.

Evocative interventions come from (and address themselves to) the withdrawal-sensation-awareness part of being. What I mean is that presence stimulates unknown parts of oneself, parts not yet fully sensed, described or named as awarenesses. Another's presence makes me feel my own being-here, my own validity. Presence is generally empowering.

Provocative interventions come from (and address themselves to) the awareness-energy-movement part of our being and doing. This means that provocative interventions intend to create particular awarenesses and actions. A provocative statement coming my way mobilizes my breathing, stimulates my thinking, offers me an opportunity to do something about myself. Hopefully, both kinds of interventions lead to both intrapersonal and interpersonal contact.

In this little article, I would like to speak to a particular form of evocative power, namely, that of presence.

The dictionary mentions "spirit or ghost" under presence. Although this is far from an adequate definition of presence, it hints at that special state of being fully here with all of oneself, one's "body and soul." It is a way of being with, without doing to. Presence implies being here fully open to all possibilities when the therapists intrinsic-being-here stimulates stirrings in the deeper parts of one's own self. The therapist's presence is ground against which the figure of another self (or selves) can flourish, brighten, stand out fully and clearly.

When I experience another's presence, I feel free to express myself, to be myself, to reveal any tender, vulnerable parts, to trust that I will be received without judgment or evaluation. My therapist's presence allows me to struggle with my own inner conflicts, contradictions, problematic questions, paradoxes--without feeling distracted by leading statements or overly determined questioning. My therapist's presence allows me to confront myself, knowing that I have a wise witness.

What Presence Is Not

Presence is not a way of posturing or self-conscious posing or strutting before another.

Presence is not style.

Presence is not charisma. Charisma asks for attention, admiration. Charisma calls to itself, while presence "Calls to the other." Charisma is a figure competing with another figure, while presence is ground, "asking to be written on."

Presence is not posed religious humility (which is really a form of secret pride).

Presence is not polemic. It does not take sides. It sees wholes.

Presence does not compete.

Presence is not flamboyant or dramatic.

Development of Presence

Rarely, therapists have appeared who simply always had presence. They seem to have been born that way. Most people acquire presence through the continual pounding of time, time which reminds them again and again how much there is to learn and how little they know. Presence is the acquired state of awe in the face of an infinitely complex and wondrous universe.

To acquire presence, one must learn many things--and then cast them away. To learn presence, one must give oneself fully away. (A metaphor comes to mind of a person who worked hard all of his or her life to acquire many riches--only to discover that the greatest pleasure is to give them away.)

Presence comes easier when one has already received approval and affirmation--when one's cup is full and one no longer needs it from anyone.

Presence is easier to experience when one learns to live with other people's pain or disappointments without having to save or rescue them.

Presence often comes when one is seasoned and one's hot longing has cooled down to a kind of warm glow my therapist's presence illuminates me.

How To Be Present

When the therapist is in a state of presence, his/her vision is peripheral and diffuse. In this state, one's breathing is deep, full, even. One's sense of time is slow and measured. One's body/self is heavily grounded. One sees wholes rather than particles. One does not "care," in the sense that one is not overly attached to the content of the client's stories.

The therapist's presence offers the client an opportunity to explore his/her own boundaries (because the therapist's boundaries are so clear, simple and unintrusive).

Finally, the therapist's presence is like sunshine--some people are developmentally ready to use it--they can "metabolize it," while others don't know that it exists and continue chattering away as if the most important part of the experience is the story of their week rather than an opportunity for a profound encounter with another. What the therapist does when this occurs is to use his/her provocative side. For example, to say, "When I listen to you, I imagine the cackling of chickens..." Perhaps at another time we can talk about provocative interventions.

1998

1973

1976

5

Notes to a Student on Making an Intervention

January 1999

Follow what happens in the other with utter faithfulness. It is all there. All that you need is in the space between you. In your response, beware of embellishing what you already stated simply.

As you watch and listen, allow yourself to see and hear every gesture, every nuance of the other's being--take it all in with pleasure.

Don't rush into responding or "helping" prematurely. Sit with the other. Quiet is lovely. It allows the other to unfold his or her thoughts and gestures in the presence of your witnessing with respect and (even) reverence. In this way, the other becomes an object of contemplation, a "mantra." Your compassionate being becomes a process of healing in its own right. Sometimes your words may actually interfere, or distract the person from this healing process.

While you sit, fill yourself with memories, images, associations, reminiscences, sentiments, yearnings… but don't part with them. (Let yourself burst with pleasure… the pleasure of concentration and a receptive sense that the other is giving you gifts).

For years, you have studied human nature, human illness and suffering--it's all there inside of you--yet the most sophisticated response is the simplest, not the most complex. People change because they feel seen, heard, understood for what they are. There are no techniques, there are no pre-arranged answers to the other's story.

You ruminate as you listen. You hear many voices in your head yet you remain silent. The voices clamor for expression and you subdue them. You let your inner fire build to the right temperature--

like a kiln--to eventually say what is salient. You prepare to throw most of the peripheral ideas and images into the garbage bin so as not to cloud the other person's awareness.

Then, in the right moment of silence... when the other is receptive and eager to learn, you speak your thoughts dispassionately, yet lovingly.

1990

6

Synthetic Thinking

1986

We are living in an age of therapeutic specialization. Emphasis is on individual creativity and innovation, perhaps even improvisation, where a kind of grass-roots eclecticism is born of each practitioner's efforts to accommodate both his/her own need for survival in the consulting room and the desire to respond to the needs of clients.

Thus we have the "thinking" therapies, the "feeling" therapies, the conditioning, the psychoanalytic, the transactional, the systems-oriented couple and family therapies, the group therapies. There are the Reichians, the neo-Reichians, the Rolfers, the Alexander and Feldenkrais people, and the hypnotists. There are the existentialists, Rogerians, transactional analysts, behaviorists, and there are the laser beamers who offer change for the price of a short trip through one's neurolinguistic software; here one can bypass awareness altogether and find, at last, some temporary relief from life's daily stress.

They are all here, thriving and accommodating people's needs for clarity, expression of feeling, muscular relaxation, muscular relearning, movement, and the realignment of adhesively demoralized muscle groups.

Process Intervention

What do I do, as a Gestalt therapist, when sitting with someone? What do I take in? What model do I construct inside of me to manage a meaningful intervention?

I see, for one thing. I see a man sitting before me, leaning forward, talking passionately, his chest turned inward. I see this dark-eyed, delicately-formed man trying to make sense of his experience as best he can.

I hear his smoker's voice, his vocal chords straining in the upper ranges. I can hear his chest straining. I can hear his breath.

I can choose to smell and to touch him.

I am aware of his language, his boy-child fantasies, his nervous habit of repeating favorite words. I am aware that, at that moment at least, he is fully invested in being right here with me. I am aware that there are two of us here with an army of other characters "standing" behind each of us (our parents, uncles, aunts, teachers, friends), egging us on, criticizing, making pronouncements and demands, praising, asking questions, and so on.

I can focus, if I wish, on his "illness," his pain and discomfort. Or I can focus on his resourcefulness, his competence, his good looks. Or I can keep all of that in mind.

The sheer quantity of data confronting me--if I see and hear and smell and touch and analyze and ponder this person--is overwhelming. Thank God, my client likes to think things out. Perhaps I'll join him there. Thinking clearly is something I can give.

But the moment I respond to his words alone, I don't see him as clearly: my vision of him is filtered by his concept of himself or diagnostic pondering about him. It is as if both of us become two little black boxes attached to a vocal apparatus. One's eyes become glazed with insights. I join the client's linguistic perspective, landing myself in the tracks of his train, getting hitched in like a horse to the wagon of his perceptions. In the meantime what happens to his chest? What happens to his mother and father "standing" behind him? What happens to the "us" in the room? How can we manage all that without becoming scattered or confused?

I can construct a picture of this person that can include all of him in this moment. I begin to ask myself: What is his theme? What is his story line? What data are useful in making a meaningful picture of this man's being here with me?

When I integrate his story, his voice and language, his way of leaning toward me, the strain in his neck and his desperate staring at me, what strikes me is a kind of pleading, as if he is begging me. Within this theme I look at him again, and I begin to highlight some things that I observed randomly just a moment ago: his arms moving toward me, his voice asking for something, his whole head tilting forward on its thin neck. In my reverie I see a baby bird with its mouth open, begging its mother for a worm. Where is mom? If there is a beggar, where are the characters who had a lot but refused to give to him?

Metaphor

He is saying something about asking his boss to let him "come here once a week at 3 p.m." So I say to him, "Ron, I experience you as begging me as you talk," and I suddenly have organized a myriad of seemingly disconnected data together. He responds by remembering his mother begging his father not to travel so much. He stops suddenly and asks a question. He then grows quiet. He looks sad. His eyes moisten. I see all of this and, after some preparatory work, ask him to position himself in this room as if he were a real beggar. He considers the idea for a moment and decides to try it.

The moment he begins to move out of his chair, his knees bend and he moves stiffly, like an 80-year-old man. "There may be a beggar inside of me, although I generally act proud--reminds me of Uncle Melvin. Melvin looked as if he had always been old. That's a little bit how I feel now. I feel I don't have, I'll never have, I won't deserve it even if I get it… I am doomed to plead and never feel entitled!"

After some experimentation with being Uncle Melvin, he stops. Sitting on the floor, he begins to cry quietly. "I lost my pride," he whispers. Soon his belly is constricting with spasms of deeper wailing. I sit down next to him while he experiences the mourning of a lost part of his himself. Much later, in the next session, he tells me once again how his body has felt as a beggar, and I wonder aloud about how he might look as the "prideful one" passing by and not bothering to toss a nickel to himself. What would happen to his shoulders and chest and knees and pelvis?

What kind of vision is able to organize itself around another's wholeness? It is a vision of process. It is a vision of the metaphors we experience of that person which he can't see himself because he is busy with his earnest commitment to his story.

How do we find this process intervention? We have to go away from him, tear ourselves away from the things he sees, and yet stay with him at the same time. We have to get in to our hardness--where he can't reach us, where we can construct uncompromisingly a fresh image of this vision in front of us.

In momentarily "turning away" from our client, we make it most possible to join him at a "kernel place," a "seed place" where his awareness has not yet traveled. This time we join him with a metaphor.

Where does the metaphor of a beggar come from? Is the beggar all his? Of course not: he is the beggar I saw in the alley in old Jerusalem, he is the beggar I read about in a novel, he is the beggar inside my childhood where, during the war, I dared to step forward to beg for chunks of moldy bread.

I tell him about his beggar, as an expert beggar whose chest still wants to collapse, whose shoulders want to draw in to protect my heart, whose knees want to collapse into the pose of an ancient Jewish man.

Existentially we are both beggars at this moment. I, the "senior beggar," welcoming him into an old fraternity, and he, the "junior beggar," who appeared to have temporarily escaped his misery by placing himself in the world of a corporate manager-trainee.

If we construct a "process picture" of him, made of his words, his voice, his physical choreography, his way of gazing sadly, then that picture, that idea, that metaphor will "pull for" seeing a part of wholeness. The metaphor, in this case, will organize his experience into an eye-opening insight that will depart from his own ego-syntonic small Weltanshaung and thrust him into an inner place where he once lived and where his whole body and soul seemed to be living. For example, he remembers a scene in his childhood when he begged his father to take him along to work--he visualizes his father wearing a dark winter overcoat, turning away from him and walking out alone into the cold Russian morning.

The story he tells is an old story for him. If you engage him there--literally there in his lively past--you will join his cast of characters. If you stand aside and look at him again and again with the fresh wonderment of a child, you might see the beggar, the murderer, the wise old man, or a trickster, or a young child asking for candy. Your own story line, evolving from the experiences of your inner life as well as his lively image, will create a play that may reorient his view of himself.

Building The Process-Self

There is no way we can do body process Gestalt therapy without having created for ourselves a rich and layered picture of our own lives. Process body work can only come from a therapist who is living his/her process. A long time ago, Carl Rogers constructed a model of process awareness in which one of the central concepts was congruence: congruence between what is expressed, for example, and what is experienced within. Congruence between doing and being. Congruence between feeling and thinking.

The therapist's own therapy requires her/him to live fully. The good therapist is a well-lived teacher. All this living, this richness, comes back into the consultation room and we work on congruence between what was experienced and what is actually felt.

So metaphors, and the sense of what is thematic for the other, do not come out of the air. They come out of the thickness of one's literate being--out of one's inner sense of poetry, vividness of imagery, lively encounter with the world, sheer curiosity, and the courage to make something extraordinary out of the simple or to make something simple out of the seeming complexity of another person's expression. The metaphor then comes out of this inner "blood learning" that is finally ripe enough to put into language and come out of one's mouth-plainly, simply, boldly--without pretense or pompousness.

1995

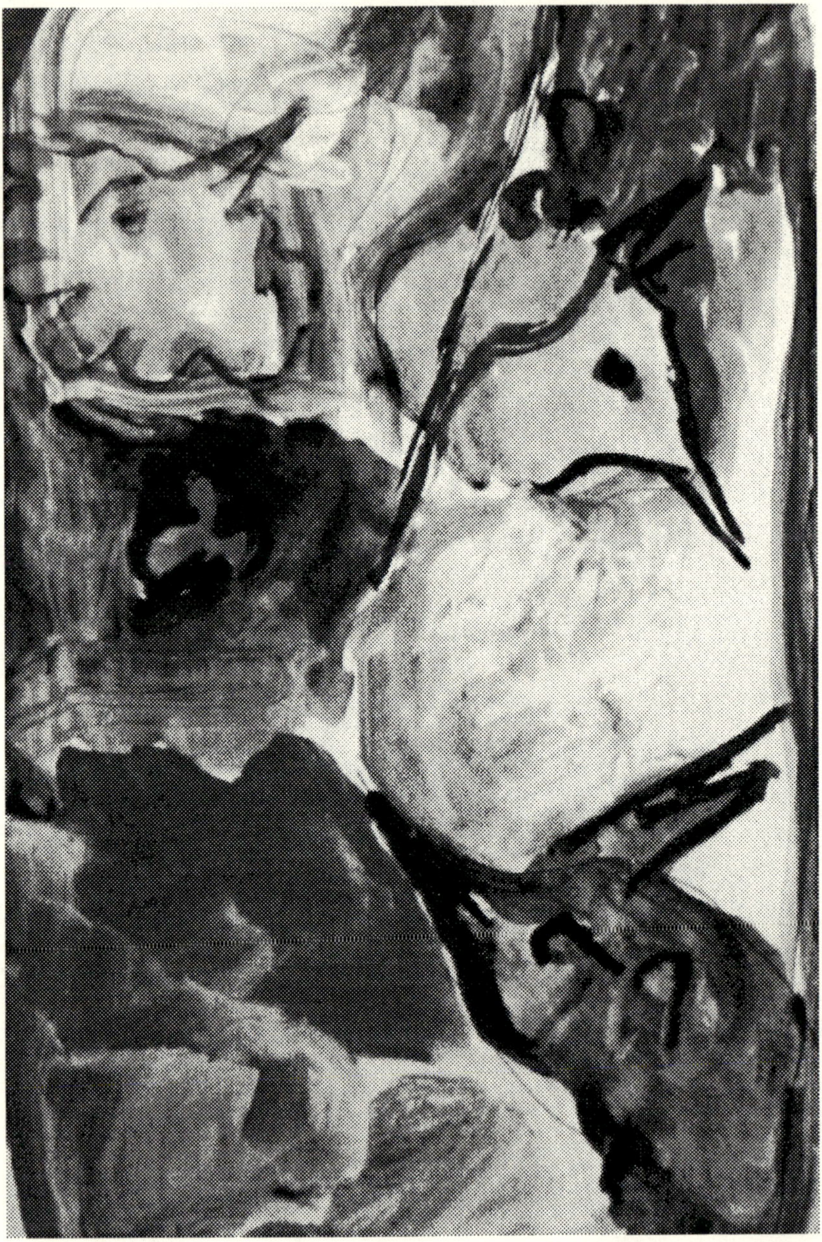

1997

7

Phenomenology of the Here & Now

1972

In a Harvard talk many years ago, e.e. cummings (1971) said to his audience:

> ...You haven't the least or feeblest conception of being here and now, and alone, and yourself. Why (you ask) should anyone want to be here, when (simply by pressing a button) anyone can be in fifty places at once? How could anyone want to be now, when anyone can go whening all over creation at the twist of a knob?... As for being yourself--why on earth should you be yourself; when instead of being yourself you can be a hundred, or a thousand, or a hundred thousand other people? The very thought of being oneself in an epoch of interchangeable selves must appear supremely ridiculous.

Cummings (1971) then wisely cautions his listeners: "...remember one thing only: that it's you--nobody else--who determines your destiny and decides your fate. Nobody else can be alive for you nor can you be alive for anyone else..."

The term "phenomenological" implies that psychophysiological process which one experiences as uniquely one's own; adding the dimensions of here and now gives these personal phenomena existential immediacy: I am this person, Joseph, sitting on this bed, propped up on two pillows, feeling the support thereof, intently scribbling notes on a small pad held in the left hand against my right knee... I feel a kind of special clarity in my head and the light here is very crisp, the sort of light I experience in the late summer afternoon when my vision seems to outline all the intricacies of the world around me. These ongoing phenomena (and more) constitute my world. When I die, that is, when my awareness permanently ceases, the whole Josephian world will be forever finished--and phenomenologically, the world will come to an end.

In recent years the term "here and now" has been used almost as a shallow slogan, a demand for extracting the other person's immediate experience as if he always experiences the choice of sharing himself, of handing what he feels to others on a golden platter using a few briskly descriptive words. Carl Rogers (1942) pointed out long ago that the phenomenological world is the experienced world; I am what I experience myself to be in this moment and if you ask what I feel right now,and I say "nothing," you can safely assume that in this moment I live in a world colored by "nothing," that I feel "nothing" inside me, or that what I do experience within I interpret to have a value of "nothing" in my communication with you. And so instead of respectfully understanding the nothing of another person's experience, we tyrannically press him for more, as if he never responded to our question.

In existential therapeutic circles the phenomenological here and now seems to be changing from that which compels my experience in this moment to a twentieth-century reverse puritanism that implies immediate satisfaction of needs, that implies a system of situational ethics , and a system that has little insight into human blockages resistances, and levels of awareness. These matters need clarification.

Sensation

Experiencing the here and now begins with sensation. In the organism with a small cerebral cortex., the sensory moment-to-moment function is primal as the cognitive process does not become conceptually elaborated. Not so in the person, sensory experience is automatically named and cognitively elaborated, and even embellished: "I see a light. It is a yellow light. It streams directly downward and upward from a table lamp with a matted glass base shaped like a holiday whiskey decanter. The lamp has an off-white paper shade... It is ugly. I don't like it. I want to get rid of it..." and so on.

Generally speaking, we forget that our language has sensorial roots, that our words stem from concrete experiences. What happens is that we begin to treat words as if words themselves are the prime experience. The pedantic (or casual) manipulation of concepts, abstractions, removes, alienates us from the immediate impact of a personal reality. To be in sensorially concrete contact is difficult in an increasingly automated world in which one is constantly distracted by second-hand cognitive noise and, in the process, rendered passive.

Exploring oneself sensorially is an active process of directing one's attention in a simple, childlike fashion: "Now I sit bent over the pad. My weight rests on my behind and the right calf on the edge of the bed. The left hand is holding on to the pad with thumb on top. The red, white and blue watch strap jumps into my eyes as I glance at it--it cuts across the wrist, dividing it in half. Now I feel my heart pounding with excitement as if I discovered something important. Now I want to lean back. There are tingles in my toes. I feel alive." The sensory exploration is active and enlivening of the self in the moment.

Time

Temporally, phenomenological reality always exists in the present (Perls, Hefferline, & Goodman, 1951).

Even in terms of my most profound and clear awareness, memory, and anticipation I have no way of experientially living my own yesterdays and tomorrows. I am temporally anchored to this (ongoing) moment. Anchored with this body that is now resting on a chair, with the things I hear (windows rattling in..the wind) with the visual experience of this page I am writing on, with the pulsing of my heart, and so on. Images of yesterday are tinted by this nowness--they are like postcards pasted in an album, an audio-visual reference library in my head; mere aboutnesses. As e.e. cummings put it,

"...anyone can go whening all over creation..." The whens of our lives are devoid of a pulse, of a liveliness especially when we try to verbalize them. We can pump life into the whens by re-enacting them now as if they are now taking place. The memory comes to life when it is sensorially and muscularly acted out and brought into the phenomenal present (Reich, 1942; Zinker, 1971). We can enliven a fantasy or a dream or an anticipation in the same way. But these reenactments become present events and are not to be confused with the actual events that took place or are about to happen. The reenactment is inseparably fused with this me that sits in this room writing and knowing myself in a momentarily special way.

Space

Spatially, my experience, my reality, takes place here where I am (Perls, Hefferline, & Goodman, 1951). The range of my "here" is determined by the phenomenal space I occupy and by the range of my senses and instruments that can extend my senses (electron microscope, radio telescope, etc.). In actual experience I make the thing sensed come dynamically into my being. If I am clearly in touch with something in space, the distance between me and my object; choice is phenomenologically foreshortened; it is as if the object is experimentally on top of me." And the dynamic point at which this sensation and I touch is called the contact boundary (Perls, Hefferline, & Goodman, 1951). An object that has a negative valence for me may be spatially pushed away and even visually contracted; the other person complains, "There is such distance between us." A psychotic girl who became very threatened by a therapy group complained that everyone looked "very tiny and far away." She left the room to follow up her experienced safe distance and finally withdrew from the workshop altogether; a position of optimum safety for her. The phenomenological here and now, therefore, represents a highly personal sensorially-anchored experience at this moment in time and at this place where I am.

Process

Within the realm of psychology, phenomenology is the uninterpreted study of the ongoing, ever-changing nature of human experience. Our personal actuality is ordinarily not static. It is never experienced segmentally or as a discrete point in time. I am constantly in process. My experience has a continuous, ongoing, everchanging quality. My ordinary propensity is to go on, to continue. It is, in fact, the characteristic of all living things: that they move in a temporal-spatial process. Life only knows itself and has an inclination to perpetuate itself.

The ordinary state of affairs for the normal organism is to fluidly move from a state of need arousal to a state of need satisfaction and from tension to relaxation from figural attention to homogenized disinterest. Moreover, the well-functioning person lives comfortably in the changing flow of his experiencing; the person is the ongoing process itself and does not experience his or her self as a static object (Rogers, 1958). It is under circumstances of disturbance, of conditioned inhibition, of pathology that one interrupts one's flow, segments one's behavior, freezes one's fluidity. In this case the individuals psychological life is in a state of incongruence where there is a considerable discrepancy between one's behavior and one's awareness (Rogers, 1958).

Resistance

All movement engenders resistance. Since experience is in constant flow, it too takes place against an inner resistance. This inner resistance of mine I experience as a reluctance to change my own ways of doing things, of behaving as I typically behave in everyday life. I take comfort in the me that has constancy. I also take comfort in my flow, but this constant change in me needs to move at a rate which is safe and clearly lubricated for me, a change which enhances the experienced me.

Resistance, unfortunately, is a term that connotes an external observation of my state of reluctance. Although I may be observed to resist some behavior, an idea or attitude or some way of looking at things, my own experience is that I am acting to preserve, maintain, and enhance my self, my psychological integrity. And what appears to you, on your observing surface, as a casual reluctance to change, may be an inner crisis for me, a fight for my life. This is the phenomenological definition of resistance, a definition that stresses the validity of the person's inner experience, his inner life (Rogers, 1942, 1961, 1958).

A few comments at the level of "plumbing" may be helpful here. My process of being and experiencing is constantly colored by the state of my needs and their frustration/satisfaction cycle. As a highly complex and easily programmed organism, I can learn to block my own need satisfaction. This blocking can occur at every level of the ingesting and assimilating process: including my sensory imputs, glands, and other internal organs, muscles, and various other vital, supportive functions like respiration. This blocking also occurs on the cortical level in the form of ruminations, obsessions, repetitious stereotyped thoughts, ad infinitum. This is what is meant by fixation and it is understood that fixation blocks the continuous development of the organism.

All psychopathology may be thought of as an extensive and often chronic interruption of the temporal-spatial process by which the organism gracefully moves to fulfill its full range of needs. The person is not robbed of his integrity; his integrity, his experiencing merely changes to accommodate this halted state of affairs, a condition which Kurt Goldstein (1963) described beautifully. Crippled behavior has its own special characteristics, and what appears "sick" to us, is a state of accommodation to blockage in the other person. I develop a stiff muscle in my neck. Quite naturally I find myself holding my neck rigidly to lessen the pain. I develop a "stiff neck" with the rest of my body accommodating itself to my neck. I walk stiffly in the street and someone sees me walking like a "zombie," but I know that as long as I walk this way I am relatively free of discomfort.

Even though the human organism is complex, its hardware, its neurons, and other cells are discrete and finite. To the degree to which human hardware (software) is manipulable, conditionable, and capable of relatively permanent storages of information, to that degree it has the tendency to retain its own functional stability. The organism perpetuates its specific way of functioning. Therefore, one of the central polarities of our existence is of stability versus change, the need to know versus the fear of knowing. The human organism is a habit-bound, behaviorally-repetitive being constantly struggling to improve its lot and modify its future. Much of our energy is used up in the tension between these two forces. And any technology which intends to modify behavior must deal with these polar resistance phenomena as being in the foreground of behavior. It stands to reason, therefore, that no matter if we deal with the "cooperative" or the "resisting" sides of the organism, we have a tendency to move toward its motivational center. All parts and forces in the organism are integrally connected structurally and functionally such that each minute part leads us toward a fuller sense of the whole.

It would seem that all fluid psychophysiological processes include polar forces of the particular phenomenon under consideration. All fluid movement, for example, involves intricate cooperation of opposing muscle groups. If it were not so, a person would become gelatinous and, like an amoeba, incapable of highly differentiated activity.

Ownership

Actuality as I experience it is my actuality. No one else can experience my inner life for me. The sensitive person may express what he or she experiences when with me. This experience of his or hers may touch something very close to me. But if one were to make an interpretation of the "real" meaning of my statement or behavior, then one would lose the purity of my experience as it is concretely revealed to me at this moment. Such a person removes their self from me by utilizing what Perls (1969) called the "computing function." Interpretations aside, the significant point here is that I am the sole owner of my phenomenological life. The old song, "You made me love you, I didn't want to do it" is out of line with our view--no one makes us do what we do and no one else can be held responsible for our behavior. The existential philosophical view stresses this point very strongly. (This is no coincidence since phenomenology is the basic method of investigation used by the existentialist philosopher. Phenomenology is a language of understanding the human predicament as mathematics is a language of understanding the physical environment.)

The experiential here and now, therefore, does not exist in a vacuum but is rather owned by a self, a person, a me. It is for this reason that the gestalt therapist repeatedly asks his patient to take ownership of his statement or observation. And the manner in which all of us avoid such ownership is described in great detail in Perls's books (Perls, Hefferline, & Goodman, 1951; Perls, 1966, 1969).

Content Validity of Awareness

The content of my experiencing is as valid a datum for me as another person's experiencing is for him or her. There are no "good" or "bad" experiential phenomena. If I report my experience, "I've had a bad day today," how can someone disagree with me?

The content of my experiencing is also in constant flux, in process. If I manage not to interrupt myself, dull and uninteresting content may develop into material which is colorful, rich, exotic. The accompanying experience moves from lifelessness and boredom to excitement and exhilaration.

To stay with my internal process is an act of faith in the sense that I assume that my experience will lead toward completion and culminate in something more satisfying and fulfilling than what I started with. The longer I can stay with my ongoing awareness, the greater the possibility of heightening, expanding, deepening my awareness. It is important, however, that I not jump the gun into complex abstracting before allowing the most concrete, pre-verbal, elemental experience to come to the foreground of awareness. In such instances one may surprise oneself with a great sense of inner revelation.

The most profound discoveries or learnings take place when

the person is self directed, rather than directed by others, when he supports himself, and when his total sensory-motor organism participates in the process rather than merely his cognitive apparatus. This kind of learning can come only from a personal framework which carries a deep respectfulness for one's uniqueness, integrity, one's ongoing awareness, one's center.

I have endeavored to clarify the meaning of the phenomenological here and now in terms of the sensory origin of awareness and considerations of time, space, process. Resistance to growth, as well as concepts of ownership and of the fundamental validity of content were also related.

What remains is the need to integrate these notions in least a general framework of theory as well as methods of psychotherapy.

Theory

Because phenomenological matters constitute the raw data of human experience, it stands to reason that all personality theorists begin their theoretical deliberations from a phenomenological base. Sigmund Freud, for example, gathered free associations and based his findings on the nature of the unconscious partially on the content, structure and process of these associations. Freud interpreted the content of human experience rather than developing a theory of the structure and content of human experience as such. He sought underlying essences of human motivation and not the topography of human experience in its own right. Interest in the latter originated primarily in existential philosophy which was variously concerned with the ontological nature of man and his condition of being thrown alone into the world, unsupported by preconceived essences. Also, phenomenology was originally a branch of philosophy and it dealt with the problems of developing a faithful, uninterpreted description of the changing phenomena of human experience. I have already mentioned that phenomenology may be understood as a language of existential thinking in general. Briefly, such are the philosophic/theoretical roots of our current concern with the here and now. On the broadest level we can assume that such modern psychotherapies as existential analysis, ontoanalysis, client-centered counseling, and Gestalt therapy are all related to the above philosophical movements. Although the methods of these therapies are very different, they share a primary interest in the person as he or she unfolds his or her being in the world in the immediacy of the therapeutic encounter.

The Phenomenological Here and Now and Psychotherapy

I cannot speak authoritatively for ontoanalysis and existential analysis because all I have read has been on the level of philosophy and theory and not at the level of methodology. Daseinsanalyse means that analysis of the state, of being here; my impression is that this expression does not necessarily cover a concrete and behaviorally extensive working relationship in the here of the therapeutic situation itself. Daseinsanalyse appears to be basically of a psychoanalytic character. The methodological emphasis is cognitive and discursive rather than, for example, behavioral and confronting.

The purest form of phenomenological here and now therapy is Rogerian client-centered counseling (Rogers, 1942, 1958, 1961). Rogers works solely with the material presented to him by the client in the counseling situation, be it an individual or group encounter. Rogers seems to accept unconditionally and to clarify precisely what the patient expresses verbally. He works verbally with the material of the patient always in the here and now. Even discussions of historical nature appear to have this quality: “You feel now that your sister's bullying made you act in a more introverted manner in high school, is that right?” It must be very refreshing to be heard, to be accepted, and to have another person help me clarify to myself exactly how I feel right now, exactly, what I need to express. No interpretive statements are heard from the counselor and, when he ventures to move beyond the content of the patient's expression, he generally takes ownership of his statement: “When I look at you sitting like this, bent over, I feel (as you might) very sad and alone.” This seemingly simple phenomenological analysis of the person's experience is very powerful in the hands of an acutely sensitive, caring therapist.

Both of the above therapies are not behavioristic in character;

they do not generally ask the patient to modify his behavior during the therapeutic encounter. For Rogers this effort would constitute manipulation of another human being; a breaking of faith with the notion of merely being there for the other without making demands that do not originate in the client.

Gestalt therapy (Perls, 1969; Perls, Hefferline, & Goodman, 1951) is a unique example of the integration of behavioristic and phenomenological approaches. Heavily influenced by organismic views of Kurt Goldstein (1963) and Wilhelm Reich (1942; 1967), Gestalt therapy attempts to understand the individuals being here at every level of organismic functioning: "When you begin to talk about your bully sister your mouth tightens. Do you feel it?" The therapist reports his observation to the patient and may go on to suggest that the patient experiment with his tightness: "Try to talk about your bully sister while tightening your mouth even more." Having made a faithful observation of the patient's physical being in the therapy session., the gestalt therapist becomes a more active teacher using the person's organismic expression to teach him something about his feelings. This is done at the most elegant level without interpreting behavior and the therapist waits for the patient's own revelation: "When I tighten my mouth, I also clench my teeth and this reminds me of the time I bit my sister. I am just remembering how furious she made me..."

The daseinsanalysis of gestalt therapy is always in the here and now of the therapy hour and includes work with the patient's full range of psychophysiological functions. All gestalt experiments are anchored in the phenomenological life of the patient as he presents himself in the situation. Arbitrary exercises thrust on the patient (or the group)--devoid of experiential roots--are not within the realm of phenomenology and of gestalt therapy at its best because they do not carry an experiential base, a living context for the patient. It is within such a living context that the most profound learnings take place.

Such are the workings, in brief, of the phenomenological here and now within the context of several prominent psychotherapies as I understand them.

Now I am sitting here, in my underwear, at the breakfast

table, trying to think of a good punchline to wrap up the paper. I am bent over the pad and I am getting distracted by my daughters' chattering. I move to my bedroom, pad in one hand, coffee in the other, and e.e. cummings (1971) comes back to me. I would like to express the hope that I have, in part, remedied his complaint that, "You haven't the least or feeblest conception of being here and now, and alone and yourself..." And for my punchline I am going to quote the rest of his statement:

> ...and remember one thing only: that it's you--nobody else--who determines your destiny and decides your fate. Nobody else can be alive for you; nor can you be alive for anybody else. Toms can be Dicks and Dicks can be Harrys, but none of them can ever be you. There's the artist's responsibility; and the most awful responsibility on earth. If you can take it, take it and be. If you can't, cheer up and go about other people's business; and do (or undo) till you drop.

References

Cummings, E. (1971). *Six nonlectures.* New York, NY: Atheneum.

Goldstein, K. (1963). *The organism.* Boston, MA: Beacon Press.

Perls, F. (1966). *Ego, hunger & aggression.* San Francisco, CA: Orbit Graphic Arts.

Perls, F., Hefferline, R., & Goodman, P. (1951). *Gestalt therapy: Excitement and growth in the human personality.* New York, NY: Julian Press.

Perls, F. (1969). *Gestalt therapy verbatim.* Moab, UT: Real People Press.

Reich, W. (1942). *Character analysis.* New York, NY: Orgone Press.

Reich, W. (1967). *The function of the orgasm.* New York, NY: Bantam.

Rogers, C. (1958). A process conception of psychotherapy. *American Psychologist, 133*, 142-149.

Rogers, C. (1942). *Counseling and psychotherapy: New concepts in practice.* Boston, MA: Houghton Mifflin.
Rogers, C. (1961). *On becoming a person.* Boston, MA: Houghton Mifflin.
Van Den Berg, J. (1955). *The phenomenological approach to psychiatry.* Springfield, IL: Charles C. Thomas.
Zinker., J. (1971). Dream work as theatre: An innovation in gestalt therapy. *Voices, 7*(2).

Malta

Life in the sunshine
without you is cloudy...

Dinners leave me hungry.
Laughter without you is a circus...

Watching lovers kiss looks vulgar...

"Racy" novels are dull...

....

Where are you, my love?

J.Z., 6/4/98

A Mission:
The Soul of a Man

I

It was only in his older years that he began to touch the earth, and to taste the salt of the ocean. He began to feel in the marrow of his bones: "this is it!" You've squandered most of your life hiding, being self-indulgent, having few friends, staying aloof from life... It had to be so. Fear was always in the ground. From time to time his yearnings would override his fear--but never fully.

II

I live in a small village in New England. I have a few friends and people say "hi" to me. I take a walk or drive to the library to get some books or video tapes.

My work is not a daily drudge but comes in blocks of time often out of town--sometimes in town. This particular week I worked with my colleagues and students for seven half days. During breaks we walked on the beach--ate together--or worked on my short stories.

III

I have two or three close friends, I visit them or they come to see me. We are intimate friends--we raise important questions about each other, about life, or about the films or plays we see. There is (sometimes) physical closeness and a great sense of safety.

IV

I feel my aging. Even though I walk a lot or bike and don't overeat, I am slowing down. I take medications. I don't sleep as deeply... One of my comforts in life are the visits of my daughters, their husbands and babies--In the summer I love to play with my grand-kids on the beach or in the woods. We paint together on the deck... We make a mess together--it is great!

V

Even though my body is slower, my images are of lively dancing: of being limber and joyful--I laugh more. My yearnings for eternal love and closeness are always there in my heart...

VI

I had a dream. As I walked alone at the edge of the rain forest, a female panther leaped out of the woods and took me away forever...

J.Z., 1996

8

On Grandparently Love

Winter 1976/1977

In the creative process, as in falling in love, we contact our sweetness, longing, powerful intention, and profound thoughtfulness. Arthur Rubinstein once said, "Playing the piano is like making love, it fills me completely with joy."

Authentic love for another is experienced as ecstasy in the very being of the other, as rejoicing in the loved one's very existence. It is non-manipulative, non-clinging, non-demanding. We let the other be. We do not wish to violate his unique human integrity. The "purest" kind of love (pure not in the Puritanical sense of being clean, but in the sense of prerequisite clarity of rejoicing in the other's being) involves the total experience of the internal tension or energy which is part of one's responsiveness to the loved one.

Thus, we can speak of love as a kind of creative tension. "Staying with" this tension and letting it permeate one's whole being is an enormously difficult task to accomplish, particularly since our society has a tendency to sell canned pleasure for immediate satisfaction.

My love for the client is apageic--more a feeling of good will toward humanity than a romantic, sentimental or possessive love. I seek my client's good, whether I like him or not. Agape love for me is thoughtful, prudent, just, benevolent, gracious. The term "brotherly love" has been used in this relation. My own image is of "grandparently love." Unlike a parent who directs his children passionately and sometimes egoistically, my grandparent asks for nothing, yet takes pleasure in learning, observing, and understanding the life experiences of another just as it is. When I experience my love passionately, as a parent, I am leery of losing my perspective and objectivity in clearly perceiving my client.

Grandparently love from me, the counselor, engenders trust. Because the therapeutic process often deals with the most vulnerable parts of the person, trust must always be there for both parties to allow the unfolding of their feelings. It is this "love" in all its forms, which lubricates the creative process between client and therapist.

Yet one does not have to love someone to respectfully attend to that person. As Martin Buber (1962) put it, "One cannot command that one feel love for a person, but only that one deal lovingly with him." And so must the therapist act lovingly with his client.

When I am there for the other
a quietness flows within,
a sweet stillness.
I am engrossed in a prayer,
witnessing another life unfolding.
I am an ancient woman
weaving cloth
for the grandchild.

The experience of feeling loved is one of acute receptivity, of taking in the gift of the other. It necessitates readiness to let the other person penetrate one's deepest stratum; it requires openness and lack of defensiveness and suspiciousness that the loving person will be injurious. In the experience of letting the other person love us, we willingly take the risk of being hurt. The fact that the loving other has the power to hurt (to reject) and chooses not to, gives the experience a sense of magnetism.

When we feel totally loved by someone who really "matters," the ecstatic receptive experience makes us feel beautiful, perfect, graceful, profound, and wise (Maslow, 1962). Our deepest, most profound stirrings of self-appreciation, self-love, and self-knowledge surface in the presence of the person whom we experience as totally accepting. It is as though we say, "When I know your total acceptance, then I can show you my softest, most penetrable, delicate, beautiful and vulnerable self" (Rogers, 1961).

My clients' "love" for me varies with their stages of development as well as with each person's specific life circumstances. Often the person projects ghosts of his past on me: I am seen as the critical or loving parent, the sadistic villain, the seducer, the teaser, the wise old man, the Christ-Rabbi, a sex object, a potential lover or spouse. As Freud pointed out long ago, psychotherapy is in some ways a working out the client's perception of the therapist.

At a higher level of development the client can appreciate and love me in the same grandparently way in which I strive to experience him. At the most advanced levels of the relationship, both people take turns grandparenting; each uses his individual competence to enhance the life of the other. Said Buber (1962), "When a man is singing and cannot lift his voice, and another comes and sings with him, another who can lift his voice, the first will be able to lift his voice too. That is the secret of the bond between spirits."

References

Buber, M. (1962). *Ten rungs: Hasidic sayings.* New York, NY: Shocken Books.

Maslow, A. (1962). *Towards a psychology of being.* Princeton, NJ: Van Nostrand.

Rogers, C. (1961). *On becoming a person.* Boston, MA: Hougton-Mifflin.

9

Polemics, Systems and the Nature of Interventions

July 1993

The most primitive (and most dangerous) thinking is categorical/monolithic thinking. That includes polemic thinking: that which espouses one polarity only--when a person knows what is good or evil; what is good for his or her patient; what is the right path for European economy and so on. That person is in denial of the multiplicity of voices in the world. Polemic voices give simple answers which imply simple solutions and fast, uncomplicated steps to solve complex issues.

I believe that polemic is developmental. Children learn that hitting is "bad" or saying "thank you" is good. Young children may get confused when someone hits them or when "thank you" feels silly because the gift given them is distasteful or "scary."

There are some words to keep in mind:

Polemic: implies making war; to "kill" your opponent.
Polarity: the presence of two opposed tendencies.
Politic(s): to be prudent; to govern (from many voices).
Categorical Authority: not as in category but as a statement of authority.
Monolithic: singularly definitive.
Middle Ground: where polarities mingle and integrate.
Dialectics and Dialogue: the first is dialogue of polarities.
Pluralistic/Diversified: different approaches from a variety of places.

In Gestalt theory, as well as in Jungian work, polarities are opposing forces within the person or even between persons--when each represents a certain "type" (e.g., feeling vs. thinking) or archetype (animus and anima). The most famous example was the one used by Fritz Perls: "top dog" vs. "underdog."

Polarities are convenient earmarks or simplifications of complex field phenomena. In psychotherapy, they allow for simple divisions of complex conflicts. Polarities imply dialogues in which the two sides or two parties seek a solution that is more or less gratifying to both parties. This is certainly different from polemics.

The term "polemic" derives from the Greek "polemikos" which is the adjective meaning "of or for war" and this, in turn, derives from "polemos" or war. In a polemic, the participant already knows what side he or she stands on and knows what kind of results are wanted: he or she wants to win! The person has hardened his or her heart against the opponent and isn't looking to learn anything new about the other.

Polarity-driven dialogues are explorations in which each side can be playful and open. Polemic-driven opponents have hardened themselves in their positions and will see to win through tactics and strategies. Polemics are out to kill their opponents while polarity dialogues are out to solve their mutual problems.

Introjected polemics result in suicidal ideation (and authoritarian cognition) while introjected polarities may lead to either conflict, lack of clarity, or to a source of clarification and resolution.

Systems

Systems are complex phenomena that have a boundary. Open systems convert energy from the environment and dissipate it by doing "work." They have permeable boundaries through which energy exchanges travel. Closed systems have rigid, thickened, brittle boundaries, often tending to be "minds-in-stasis," and have little or no growth.

Persons with more or less rigid boundaries are both disconnected from their inner (sluggish) process as well as not in dialogue with the environment. These include young infants, severely brain-damaged persons and psychotics. Process is almost no process at all in that there is no movement or learning; no increase in complexity. Structure is static and colorless.

Persons with permeable boundaries, "open persons," are in constant process, constant change, require constant replenishment of energy, and are connected to themselves and others. They tend to grow in complexity and evolve their problems into higher and higher levels of abstraction or human concern.

This is true of all systems: intrapsychic, dyadic, families, clans, organizations, and countries. Couples and families that have "closed" boundaries tend to be retroflected. Their energy is unexpressed and kept static. They are difficult to help because their boundaries are so rigid and brittle and consequently can't metabolize a therapeutic encounter. They are generally sent to a clinic and have a difficult time asking questions, asking for help, or learning from the therapist. They listen respectfully, often politely accept or reject advice, and then go on their way. They are lonely, frightened, and isolated from friends and neighbors.

Open system persons, couples, and it may be problematic if they are too open. Lack of boundaries allows for poor protection and easy intrusion and injury. Often these are poor, disorganized families who are easily manipulated by outsiders and have little skill to take care of themselves or take care of each other for that matter. Healthy open systems--those that are elastically bounded--can talk to one another, help each other, support differences (inner differentiations), engage in dialogue, and reach to their friends and community for connection.

On a personal, intrapsychic level, there is a free exchange between differentiated parts of the psyche and these persons can be approached at different levels and will make an effort to respond and, if not, to ask questions.

* * *

Because of the explosion of general systems theory, field theory, theories of chaos and complexity, and of both molecular and cosmic physics, it has become increasingly difficult to focus on an individual's inner workings without factoring in the social matrix and organismic "soup" in which he or she lives. Let me take the classic resistances to contact as an example to illustrate this idea.

In the old days, we saw someone who introjected as someone who swallowed whole. Yet, introjection is by definition an interactional phenomenon. That is, one introjects from someone else and this "someone else" has certain characteristics: he or she doesn't ask questions, tends not to wait long enough to hear answers, and tends to force feed ideas, feelings, etc. That "someone else" is not in dialogue with another. By the same token, the introjector is not an innocent victim. He or she reinforces the force feeing by taking too long to answer, by being passive-aggressive, and, most importantly, by not objecting or refusing what is offered to them. Introjection is thus a social field phenomenon in which two or more persons cooperate to create a shove-and-swallow dance, a dance in which swallowing is the rule and learning is impossible on all sides.

We can find similar interactional patterns in the case of projection, retroflection, and confluence. Each case is interactional. Each case is, in fact, a process, not a static, immobile phenomenon. All of us are in motion, in process, together or separately.

Projectors find partners who accept projections without objecting to or correcting the projection, or find partners who don't say easily what they feel, what they want, and what they don't want.

A retroflecting person experiences discomfort and does not ask for help. His or her partner witnesses the discomfort and doesn't offer help. They take turns suffering and feeling utterly abandoned. Confluent partners agree not to rock the boat; being challenging or provocative is simply against the rules of their system.

Systems theory tells us that when one of us does something, it affects all of us.

Complexity and Interventions

When you watch a small system such as a couple or a family, you see and hear an incredible amount of material. It is very complex.

First, you may be attracted to what they are talking about: the content. Content is seductive as it draws you in because it often arises from conflict and disagreement; what I have called polemics and polarities. In polemic disagreement, as you recall, the persons are stuck on winning and fighting to the death. If you've faced this kind of situation, you may also recall how dismayed you were to sit in the presence of such fighting. Or, if you've been lucky, you've seen persons who were polarized; they were in disagreement but were making some effort to solve their problem. In these situations, as you continue watching, you will notice that--quite independently of content--there is process. For example, you may notice that their talk has a circular quality; they go round and round, get stuck, and then repeat themselves.

If you keep an open mind about how they talk, where they sit, who dominates, who is the "troublemaker," who is the "good one," and so forth, the data are truly overwhelming.

If you grab onto the content--the material that divides them--you may fall into the following common errors:

1. You find one side more attractive than the other (countertransference).

2. You may want to solve the problem by encouraging them to find a compromise. The weakness of this intervention is that they don't really learn anything about where they got stuck in their process and so similar conflicts will arise in future, content-laden situations.

3. You may want to teach them to talk differently. For example, teaching them to say "I want" instead of "You should." This is like giving a cancer patient a haircut instead of performing surgery.

Process and Phenomenology

So then you give up the content and simply watch them for the how of their interaction rather than the "what" of they're saying. You begin to notice patterns of process--and where they become stuck--quite independent of the polemics (or yours).

You try to make sense of repeated patterns and, at the same time, to simplify the mass of data before you.

You are probably familiar with the contact-cycle pattern as developed in at the Gestalt Institute of Cleveland. It follows the sequence of:

1. Awareness
2. Energy
3. Movement
4. Contact
5. Completion or Resolution
6. Withdrawal

These are not necessarily the only phenomena; you are free to add others. You may add resistances to contact at different levels of this cycle but interventions must be bilateral.

Let us take a hypothetical couple and watch them for a moment. They are arguing about how to run their business. She wants plans in advance--30 days in advance. He like to wait and get more information to make a decision and so they are in opposition to one another. This is the content.

Now for the process: the polemic "heats up." Her voice becomes shrill and, as it rises, he becomes stiff, rigid in his body, and more entrenched in his position.

We can tell that they are located somewhere in the energy/movement part of their interaction and that they are stuck between energy and contact. Here is what the first intervention may sound like:

"I've been watching you talk now for ten minutes. You talk well and stay with the issue (remind me about this later) but there is something else more difficult. As your voice rises and you become more frustrated, Barbara, you, Bill, get stiffer and more rigid in your body and your position. Have you ever noticed this?"

Now you have found a pattern almost devoid of content but real and easily seen again and again. You have made a pattern out of chaos; a pattern with phenomenological validity and reliability.

The couple may then question the usefulness of your observation regarding their stuckness and ask what good does knowing this do?

Here is one answer: "You see, if we get curious how you repeatedly get stuck in your process--and you learn to change that--then you will be able to get unstuck no matter if you disagree about the business or about vacations or about dinner time. If either one of you learns to change your behavior, for example, either relaxing your voice--as in your case, Barbara--or sitting back in your chair, Bill, and getting stiffened up, then you will do much better no matter what topic we deal with." As they say they are willing "to at least try it," I would then say, "Bill, this time would you be willing to sit back and try not to stiffen no matter how strident Barbara's voice becomes? And Barbara, you can try playing with your voice when Bill gets really rigid and immobile in his position."

They try it out for a few minutes and, by God, their content changes. They begin to sound more conciliatory.

When you change the process of a couple's connecting or the choreography of movement or their body stance or their voices, the system's stuckness will typically open up. And you need not necessarily use my model of awareness-contact-withdrawal. You can invent your own observation system in accordance with what stands out for you as you watch the system. For example, you may see a pattern of humor or sarcasm that interests you as when one person asks a question and the other uses sarcasm to answer. Or if one person always asks questions and the other always delivers sermons or lectures.

In a family system, you may find triangulation as when one person asks something of the spouse and a child deflects by changing the question or answering for the parent.

The main point is that you give feedback to the system about actual process material you see and hear and that you deliver this without criticism but in a matter-of-fact tone as: "You talk well together but I notice something that may interest you. Every time Mom asks Dad a question, Bobby tries to answer it for Dad. Have you noticed that?"

It is best to always support what is good first and then give your observation of the pattern-phenomenon.

Other observations may be related to the fact that they elucidate ideas and feelings well but they can't stop and savor their sense of having completed something. They can't rest but ramble on and on. This is simply what you see and you may want to support what you see by describing who said what.

The main point here is to tell the system what you observe that is simply of interest to you and that is not content-driven.

Summary of Principles

Having now discussed polemics, systems, complexity, and interventions, I will now summarize the same basic principles of pattern formation that may be useful to your work.

Principles of Pattern Formation

1. There is no linear progression in human relationships; no ordinary causes and effects; just complex interactions.

2. All events, including human relationships, are in constant process.

3. Relationships tend to triangulate.

4. No "identified patient" exists without a pattern of "unidentified patients."

5. History, albeit family or culture, is not a "story" but many events exploding "all at once" making a pattern.

6. Content is seductive and process needs careful observation and neutral feedback.

7. The individual being, even in isolation (e.g., a hermit), is in relation to others.

8. Any event anywhere in a system, small or large, affects all other events; no event can be seen in isolation.

9. Couples and families are complementary; change the mood of one member and the moods of the others change as well.

10. Reductionism is dangerous because it tends to harbor or stimulate polemic interaction and the desire to destroy the other.

11. We must face the problem of apparent paradox between autonomy and relationship. Only truly autonomous persons can have vibrant relationships. Confluent relationships kill the spirit.

12. The world is both one and also pluralistic. Events in the world must be examined as interaction between wholeness and poli-

tics. The world is made up of diverse voices yet we are all one.

13. Couples and families are dissipative structures. They tend to run out of energy at certain developmental stages. Ideal restructuring of these stages involves moving upward into higher levels of functioning.

Implications for Gestalt Therapy

1. Look for patterns in the psyche or in the larger system. The most useful patterns are based on actual, here and now observations and these are phenomenological/process-oriented: time, space, change, awareness, sensation, polarized specialization, energy, choreography of movement and location, quality of contact, nature of withdrawal, capacity to "let go" and start again, humor, and a sense of the philosophical.

2. Even in individual work, every intervention must carry a pattern of your patients' outside existence in your brain. You must have an understanding of the "soup" they are floating in.

3. In couple's work, interventions must be both systemic and complementary. Interventions to one and not the other--positive or negative--will not be beneficial to the system.

4. Understand development and what is developmentally appropriate in your intervention. Also, understand that there are exceptions to all rules and, while they can be must useful ordinarily, they are also potentially stupid and dangerous without awareness.

5. Understand and observe power discrepancies in small systems. Strong discrepancies in power can result in abusive behavior. (This true even in the largest of systems as in the case of a "landslide" victory of a politician being interpreted as a "mandate from the people" and used as a rationalization for abuse.)

6. As a therapist, you must constantly "track" your own moods, desires, conflicts, needs, and changing ideologies because the person sitting in your presence will be affected/effected by your moods.

7. Attend both to the unique voice in the psyche or system as well as the pattern of voices as a whole.

8. Never take sides or lose your boundary; balance one intervention with another.

9. Respect the system's integrity and its capacity to change on its own.

10. Support resistance while you join the system. The more you support what is, the more change will occur.

Germany

The quickened heart
pounds deep... engorging me with pain.
SELF LOATHING.
SELF RECRIMINATION.

It's how I lived LIFE and
payments are made
in regular coinage
of coagulated blood.

. . .

Times come when old, old men
relax into expressionless
drifting, empty of egoistic regrets,
empty of yearning...
Life was lived fully, thoughtlessly,
with celebration of one's pleasure and foolishness

The poet wakes from his
nightmare
and with presence of mind
etches out a line or two
with his blood-learning.

And now, eternal quiet.

J.Z., 1997

10

Rosa Lee

1963 (Published in 1966)

Excerpts from *Rosa Lee: Motivation and the Crisis of Dying*

Introduction

Many contemporary psychologists, psychiatrists, philosophers, and writers have eloquently expressed the ideas that death is a fact in human existence, that this fact tends to be denied by Western culture, that dying and death are profoundly significant incidents in the individual's life, and finally, that the phenomenon should receive greater attention in scientific investigations than it has until now.

Problems of the dying individual seem to be avoided in psychological literature, in medical literature, and by hospital personnel who come in contact with dying patients every day. It is as if scientific literature, as well as those person who come in contact with dying individuals, pronounce these individuals (and this category eventually includes all of us) as psychologically dead before they actually expire. Physicians and nurses on hospital wards, as well as families of dying individuals, often avoid discussing such problems with each other. Paucity of literature in this area is one more sign of a lack of communication on the subject.

Actually, death and its meaning in human events belong to a group of significant, often common, human experiences, all of which have been neglected in contemporary psychological investigations.

Rosa Lee Brown, 1963

Phenomena in our everyday lives the nature and meaning of which need greater study are, for example, "love," "hope," and "striving," varieties of religious experience, as well as "peak experiences" and "insight experiences."

One way of evaluating the meaning of death in human existence is to study the behavior of the individuals who are most intimately connected with it: those who are dying. Studies of dying patients that do exist--and these are mainly studies done by psychiatrists and psychologists--reflect the fact that this area is taboo in our society. The attitudes of the researchers in these studies seem to be that dying and death are inherently psychologically "bad," "negative," "deteriorating" experiences in human life. It is as though the dying individual is not given credit for his capacity to come to grips with, to reinforce his most cherished beliefs and ideas, or even to take a step forward in some way to arrive at a more meaningful picture of his life and understanding of the world that he has experienced.

The fact of the matter is, however, that great literary works, autobiographies, and news media have reported and described time and time again how individuals who have been on the brink of death, or individuals who knew they were to die in the near future, experienced the greatest insights, the greatest joys, the most important re-evaluations of their past lives; many of them achieved greater religious strength and greater love for their fellow man; they found integration, closure of their past lives and sometimes even took a step forward: they "grew." One thinks, for example, of Frankl, Myerson, Neuberger and Wertenbacker.

The purpose of this study is to investigate the possibility of growth in an ordinary, uneducated, southern woman dying of metastatic cancer

It should be made clear from the beginning that the present writer considers death to be a fact of human existence, and feels that there is little or no scientific understanding of its significance for the individual human being (or for humanity in general). It is assumed that the area legitimately belongs within the realm of scientific investigation. It is, therefore, one of the purposes of this study to fill the need for greater understanding of death as a significant variable in human existence.

Background for the Study

About four years ago I became interested in the general question of the meaning of death in human experience. As I was taking undergraduate psychology courses, many of the papers I wrote were related to answering this question; these papers dealt with the development of the child's concept of death, the child's fear of death and the treatment of this fear, and the nature of theories--such as Existentialism--which deal with death. More recently I have thought about and written on problems of counseling with the dying patient and on growth as a result of loss and crisis.

In February 1960, I was given the opportunity to work in Highland View Cuyahoga County Hospital, a hospital for chronic illnesses in Cleveland, Ohio. I felt that this was an excellent chance to acquire concrete experience with dying individuals and to formulate some realistic issues which might be explored in a formal study. At Highland View, I saw and evaluated many people who were seriously ill as part of my function as a staff psychologist there.

I attended "tumor conferences" in which physicians discussed plans for treatment of cancer patients. I was often struck by the feeling of futility that pervaded these conferences. In cases in which there was little hope of curing the patient, members of the staff working with him seemed to think of him as an individual whose life, in a psychological sense, had already ended. This is a striking example of what I have already called the "negative" approach to the dying patient.

Between February 1960 and January 1963, I established several long-term relationships with dying individuals. This study is the outgrowth of one of these relationships.

My interest in the patients I knew there was not that of a psychotherapist--a person who wants to change them--but as a student of individuals' reactions to serious illness.

One of these individuals was Mrs. L., a 77-year-old widow suffering from cancer of the breast. I saw her about once a week from

October 1960, when I met her, to April 10, 1961, the day she died. Some of initial impressions of Mrs. L. were that she denied her illness and that she found little meaning in her life and wanted to die. As I continued seeing her, these impressions were confirmed; but what most impressed me was the apparent fact that Mrs. L.'s life during these months did not seem to have much movement, that it had a static quality. She appeared to have given up the desire to change, to grow, to respond in a flowing, flexible manner to the events around her. She spoke about the weather when I met her and she spoke about the weather an hour before her death. It occurred to me that, perhaps, by using Mrs. L.'s taped talks, this quality of her personality might be confirmed. When several other psychologists listened to our interviews, they, too, were impressed by the static aspect of Mrs. L.'s life. This quality seemed to be more broad and crucial than the impression that she "denied" her illness.

A dying patient with whom I established a relationship was Miss RL, a 50-year-old paraplegic woman whose breast cancer metastasized to her lungs. Miss RL turned out to be the central figure of my study. In contrast to Mrs. L's lack of interest and inquisitiveness about her illness and its treatment, RL anxiously and actively sought information about many aspects of her condition and its treatment. She seemed to be fighting to integrate and assimilate every feature of her present situation into her life. In contrast to the static quality of Mrs. L.'s life, RL's life was dynamic and seemed to be moving in the direction of an attempt to come to terms with her present dilemma. RL was often depressed, but it was not enough to think of her simply as a depressed dying woman; what appeared more pertinent as her illness progressed was her psychological change.

I developed so a close relationship with RL that I felt I was sharing her crisis with her. She was first seen by me in February 1961 soon after her arrival at the hospital, and I saw her continuously until the day she died on July 23, 1961. During period I recorded--with her permission--31 of our talks. These recordings constituted the basic raw data of this study.

There is little question in my mind that RL was in some way influenced by me. I know that my experience with her influenced my own life profoundly in a positive direction. I learned from her that man can relinquish all the things and events which anchor him to safety. In this process, he does not begin to feel that life has no meaning, for the meaninglessness of life is the product of the anxiety to find meaning in it. Man can freely give himself to life, allowing it to permeate his sensibilities as much as sensibilities will permit.

Purposes and Conceptual Framework of the Research

The first specific purpose was related to the problem of the "nomothetic" approach in the study of the dying person. As has been illustrated in the review of the literature, the approach in the study of dying persons has mainly been that of classifying them into psychiatric diagnoses and defense mechanisms. It is felt that in using such an approach on groups of dying patients, there is a tendency to oversimplify or to dismiss issues that may be at hand, and at the same time, to lose the full richness and complexity of the dying individual's needs, satisfactions, and frustrations.

In order to cope with this first problem, a detailed longitudinal study of one dying individual's needs, frustrations and satisfactions was carried out. A single dying woman was studied from the time of her arrival at the hospital to the moment of her death, five months later, in a way designed to get as full a picture of changes in her personality as possible.

A biased labeling of the individual's behavior (through psychiatric diagnoses or defense mechanisms) was avoided by tapping a broad range of the patient's motivations, their satisfaction and dissatisfaction, i.e., a comprehensive picture of her motivations during her illness and approaching death. The identity of the individual was preserved and not squeezed into one or another category. It was considered important to study the individual as a universe, and the forces around her and within her as the population of significant variables.

The second specific purpose dealt with the problem of the "negative" approach in the study of the dying individual discussed above. RL's motivational life was followed in such a way as to allow for the discovery of personality change in both negative and positive directions: not only did I investigate "lower" need functioning but also "higher" level need functioning. The door was left open for the exploration of both phenomena under general category of psychological change associated with the patient's motivations.

Psychological change was determined by following (through an analysis of the interviews) RL's need patterns as her illness progressed. Assuming that every individual has a hierarchy of needs I studied the patterns of change in the patient's needs within this hierarchy as her illness progressed…

If Maslow's tenets are strictly followed, then it would seem that by definition a dying person cannot grow because her physiological and safety needs are progressively less well satisfied. Since her basic needs are less and less nearly satisfied, how can he possibly satisfy higher-level needs?…

Methods and Procedures

Thirty-one "open-ended" bedside interviews with the subject were carried out by this investigator; they were recorded over a period of five months during the subject's illness. These interviews were later carefully transcribed and comprise the nucleus of the present study. Each of these interviews was rated independently by two psychologists with doctoral degrees. The judges used both original recordings and re-recorded transcriptions on sixty items representing Maslow's hierarchy of needs (12 items for each need)…

Patient's History

Rosa Lee Brown was a single, 51-year-old woman. She was a heavy (273 pounds), Southern woman born in Midville, Georgia on May 31, 1910, the youngest of six children. Midville, with a population of about 680, is located about 60 miles southwest of Augusta, Georgia. It is an agricultural area of tenant farmers who raise cotton, melons, pecans, and truck farm products. Rosa Lee attended school through the fourth grade, at which time it was necessary for her to quit school and help her father, who was a sharecropper. In 1927 she became ill with polio. Never properly treated, she remained an invalid, paralyzed from the knees down, until her death on July 23, 1961.

The type of social and sexual life which Rosa Lee led in her early years is unknown except for one incident. When she was 19 or 20 years old, she gave birth to a baby out of wedlock. She said the "mishap" had occurred out of ignorance. There was a "showdown" before the whole family. Rosa Lee killed the baby because it "seemed like the right thing to do" at the time. Further information about this incident is not available, except that she became more deeply religious after this period.

Rosa Lee lived in Georgia with her parents until their deaths. Her father was a tenant farmer who was provided with living quarters and food, seeds, and tools by his landlord. He received a certain share of the value of the crop. Rosa Lee had two older sisters and two older brothers. The sex of the sixth child is not known.

Rosa Lee's mother died from cancer in 1933 at the age of 66, and her father died in 1940. He was 83. Rosa Lee and her father were both known to the Department of Public Welfare in Georgia when in May 1938 they were "certified" to receive surplus food. When her father died Rosa Lee moved in with a married sister and stayed there until the sister died in 1948. Following this she lived alone and attempted to manage a small store, but the venture did not do well. She received some help from her neighbors while living alone.

At the time of her hospitalization there was still one 83-year-old brother in Georgia, but he was ill and had nine dependents to support and could not offer any help to Rosa Lee.

In August 1953, Rosa Lee was brought to Cleveland by her widowed sister. They lived together in her sister's first-floor, front apartment in an old, dilapidated building. The rooms were very tiny, but very clean and well kept. Rosa Lee slept in the only bedroom, and her sister slept on a rollaway bed in the kitchen. There was no hot water and whenever hot water was needed it had to be boiled. Rosa Lee was able to get in and out of her wheelchair by herself, take care of her own toilet needs, dress herself, and do the cooking…

In the fall of 1954, Rosa Lee's sister went to the Cleveland

Welfare Department to apply for aid. She was earning $130 a month but when Rosa Lee came to live with her, there was hardly enough to live on, and nothing left to put away for savings. This request was denied because it was felt that Rosa Lee's sister had sufficient income to cover Rosa Lee's needs. In the beginning of the following year, Rosa Lee informed the Cleveland Welfare Department that her sister's wages had been cut and she felt that now they should be eligible for aid. Here is her letter asking for aid:

Dear Miss Drake,
You Sent Me a letter Dec. 6 told me it were any changes made in the Home For me to contact the Welfare Dept. agin. Since them my sister Hours been cut I don't have no aid. She dont earn enough to cover our expense. dont have much food in the home I have not been able to get clothes For Winter please help me

From Rosa Lee Brown

After further investigation the sisters were finally given aid beginning in July 1955.

On July 22, 1955, Rosa Lee entered St. Vincent's Charity Hospital with a diagnosis of adenocarcinoma of the right breast with metastasis. Surgery was performed and her right breast was removed. Within the following two months she had a total hysterectomy and bilateral salpingo-oophorectomy (surgical removal of an oviduct and ovary) for a fibroid uterus.

At the end of her hospitalization in December 1955, Rosa Lee was transferred to the County Nursing Home where she remained until December 1960. While in the Home she lived in a first-floor ward with a number of other women. She had a corner bed which gave her some privacy and room to manipulate her wheelchair. She spent a large amount of her time in Occupational Therapy making pillow cases, scarves, etc., for which she received one-third of the selling price when each article was sold. She apparently enjoyed her participation in these activities, and often came very early in the morning or late in the afternoon because she enjoyed the peacefulness and quiet of the therapy room in contrast to the noisy disturbance of her ward. Sometimes she would talk with the therapist; sometimes she would just sit alone on the porch.

While she lived in the nursing home, Rosa Lee made periodical requests for several items to be purchased with her own money. She was very explicit about the type of stockings she wanted, saying they must be silk because both cotton lisle and nylon irritated the skin on her legs. She also asked for slippers and special bras made for women with breast amputations. These were purchased for her, though her requests often irritated the personnel.

In May 1958, Rosa Lee also asked for new glasses because she was having headaches and could no longer work in O.T. Eight months later she received her new bifocal glasses which she said were like a "new pair of eyes."

During her last three years at the home Rosa Lee often talked of her desire to live with her sister again. Her sister had been looking for a new apartment for them because the doorways in her present apartment were too narrow for Rosa Lee's wheelchair. Since Rosa Lee's sister now had a cardiac ailment, the Welfare Department felt that it was not wise for Rosa Lee to return to live with her. Early in 1960, Rosa Lee's sister did buy an old house with plenty of space, and the question again arose whether Rosa Lee ought to move in with her sister. However, upon visiting the house and finding there would be no heat in her room or the bathroom, she agreed with the Welfare Department that the house was not suited to her needs.

In the summer of 1960, Rosa Lee said she wanted to move to the Golden Age Club, but she was told there were no openings, and they really did not have the type of room that Rosa Lee would need.

In December 1960, Rosa Lee caught a heavy cold and complained of severe chest pains. The doctor diagnosed it as pleurisy with effusion. She was sent to Metropolitan General Hospital so that her present illness could be investigated in relationship to her previous malignancy. X-rays and further examinations showed a metastasis to the right breast and also to the chest. The doctor at Metropolitan General Hospital referred Rosa Lee to Highland View Hospital for X-ray treatments, and she was admitted on February 1, 1961. Highland View accepted her for palliative care with possible conditional discharge to her sister's home or the County Nursing Home.

Prior to 1960, when Rosa Lee became seriously and painfully ill, she enjoyed being with her many friends. She was well liked at the Nursing Home by both patients and personnel. Her sister came to see her quite often, as did many people from her church.

Although completely confined to her wheelchair, Rosa Lee always tried to be as independent as possible, and did not rely on others for help. While with her family in Georgia, she did the cooking and took care of the housework. She did not seem to mind being in a wheelchair until near the end when she became to weak to move about as she had before.

Rosa Lee was of the Baptist faith, and a firm believer in God and His power to order all things. A Protestant chaplain said of her religious attitude: "She had a mature religious outlook based on a simple but sound theology." While living in Cleveland, Rosa Lee was sometimes taken to church which had a special service for sick people. A bus would transport these people and the church would have a service, dinner, and singing by a choir. Rosa Lee did not like to miss church services but sometimes found it impossible.

She had some very definite beliefs about God. When asked if she felt that she had been "singled out" by God for punishment, she replied, "Oh no! I never feels that way. I don't believe God punishes. I think it comes from the devil. God don't put sickness on anybody." She also said that God would forgive sins, although there is nothing man can do to earn God's goodness. She was quite familiar with the Bible and could repeat passages from memory. She said she read the Bible often until it became too difficult for her to see. She also enjoyed listening to three religious radio broadcasts…

Rosa Lee liked plants and enjoyed caring for them. She liked to be able to look out on trees and lawns. Working with her hands either in sewing or craft work gave her pleasure; she liked making beautiful things. She enjoyed clean jokes and showed a sense of humor to those who knew her well.

Rosa Lee was in Highland View Hospital for six months. She died on July 31, 1961 from cancer of the breast with metastasis to mediastinal lymph nodes, lungs, and pleura.

It is interesting to note that only hours before her death Rosa Lee called in the present researcher and other staff members and thanked them all for the good care she had received. She was not in great discomfort when she died, and in many respects she appeared to be at peace with herself and the world…

Excerpt from an Interview with Rosa Lee Shortly Before Her Death

Joseph: What made you... what made you feel that... for some people it is better not to know?

Rosa Lee: Well, cause I's been around some people and seen them grieve and worry over... over things that the doctor would tell them.

Joseph: Just lately, or uh...

Rosa Lee: Well, not just lately, but it's been true sometimes. Ain't been just lately, but I have been around people that worry about things that the doctor would tell 'em. But nobody's gonna see me worried about nothin' the doctor tell me... 'cause I figured out just like I do... if it's the Lord's will for me to get over it, I'll get over it. And if it's Lord's will for that to kill me it's gonna be part of it.

Joseph: And either way, how does it make you feel? How does that make you feel?

Rosa Lee: How does it make me feel to know that I'm going that way?

Joseph: Yeah.

Rosa Lee: Well, it make me feel just the same as I know I'm goin' one way, I know I've got to go... That don't make me feel bad to go that way. You get tired of sufferin'. Some things, if someday maybe you could have, you get tired of sufferin'. But to worry about you're gonna die... when you gonna die of somethin'... you gonna die of with somethin'. The only way you don't die, you don't be born. If you're ever born you sure gonna die. That's true. You must die.

Joseph: As long as you're born.

Rosa Lee: Yes, as long as you're born you're gonna die.

Joseph: The minute you're born, you're...

Rosa Lee: There's gonna be death. So long as you don't be born you won't have to die. But the minute you're born, you can just die anytime... And it don't worry me to know what I have, and to know what I'm gonna die of... that don't worry me.

Joseph: What worries you? What does worry you?

Rosa Lee: To be like I am: can't get out of bed and can't help myself. That worries me, because I like to be independent. I don't like to worry other people doing things...

Results

Agreement between the judges for each of the thirty-one interviews based on the placement of all 60 Q-Sort items was found to be highly significant.

Using wheelchair tolerance and chest X-rays (metastatic cancer changes) as indices of physical deterioration, it was demonstrated at a high level of confidence that the patient became progressively physically deteriorated with the passage of time.

On this basis, findings regarding temporal changes in the patient's needs, and their satisfaction and frustration, could be discussed in relation to a temporal factor of physical deterioration.

Physiological and safety needs were significantly more important to the subject than the other three needs. These needs had greater weight in motivating her behavior, independent of time of illness, than the other needs in the hierarchy. Physiological needs and safety needs did not differ from each other, each playing an equally dominant motivating role. At the other end of the hierarch, esteem needs and needs for self-actualization did not differ from each other, playing equally unimportant role in comparison to lower-level needs.

In terms of changes over a period of time, there was a tendency for physiological needs to become increasingly more important to the subject as her illness progressed. There was also a tendency for esteem needs to carry less and less weight in the subject's motivational life as she neared death. Changes in the other three needs during the patient's illness were not found to be significant. A significant inverse relationship was found between physiological needs and esteem needs. This provides partial evidence of psychological decline with physical deterioration, and supports Maslow's contention that when the individual becomes concerned with lower-level needs, higher-level motivation tends to suffer.

The subject's physiological needs were significantly more frustrated than all remaining needs. Safety needs were more frustrated than the three needs higher in the hierarchy. Self-actualization needs were less satisfied than love needs and esteem needs. Love needs were significantly more satisfied than all other need categories.

In terms of temporal changes on the Satisfaction-Frustration continuum, there was a tendency for the subject to become increasingly more frustrated in her physiological needs as her illness progressed. Satisfaction and Frustration of the other four needs did not change with the progression of the patient's illness.

A trend toward an inverse relationship was found between the subject's physiological needs and their Satisfaction and Frustration. More specifically, the more she was motivated by physiological needs the less satisfaction she found in the attempt to meet these needs. This result makes sense in the light of the fact that RL was dying. On the other hand, a significant positive relationship was found between the subject's needs for self-actualization and their Satisfaction and Frustration. Thus, when she was more motivated in the direction of self-actualization, she found more Satisfaction in these needs, and vice versa. A significant inverse relationship was found between physiological needs and the Satisfaction-Frustration of needs for self-actualization. This means that when physiological needs were strong (and when she was intensely ill) needs for self-actualization were more frustrated, and vice versa. This result again seems to support an earlier confirmation of Maslow's idea that self-actualization needs suffer when physiological needs predominate.

There was no significant change in the Need Hierarchy Score. This means that neither Growth nor Decline took place for the subject and that she maintained an overall stability of her needs as far as their overall upward or downward change within the need hierarchy is concerned. At the same time, a qualitative examination of the Q-Sort data pointed to some signs of Growth in the last days of the subject's life.

Discussion

Implications

The literature in this field has been characterized as being "Nomothetic" and "Negative;" it is felt that in the study of the dying human being, issues have been oversimplified and the individual person lost. The accent of research has been on the psychopathological and defensive side of reactions to the dying process.

In this research an effort was made to study one dying person in great detail over a period of time, using an "open" approach. By the "open" approach is meant that the door was left open, not only in the direction of discovering Decline, but also in the direction of discovering Growth. Because no attempt was made to "prove" or demonstrate one point of view, aspects of Decline, of Growth, as well as of stability, were discovered within the complex reactions of the subject to approaching death. On a long range basis it was found that generally RL's motivational life did not change as she was dying. At the same time there was some indication that with the increase of her physiological needs, a concomitant decrease of esteem needs took place; this relation could be described as a kind of Decline. Finally, possible aspects of Growth were discovered in RL shortly before her death in a qualitative analysis of the data. Such Growth might have been overlooked had we relied only on results of statistical tests designed to tap long range changes.

What does all this mean? Can these findings be generalized and applied to other human beings? Is this research more than just a detailed clinical study? These are questions that any practical person will raise and we might attempt to answer them partially with a quotation from a publication called *Manas*:

> Until quite recently the behavioral sciences--including history--have dealt with man as a "thing." They have given us the view that human beings are not quite real unless they exist in large

> numbers. According to this view, you can say things about man that are worth saying only if you have a statistically significant sample. The new view is that one man has enough significance in him to reveal fundamental truth about all men. A single man is not a minute sample of "something else" called the human race. A single man is some sense IS the human race. Or you could say that every man is an archetype of every other.

Much has been written about the growth and self-actualization of great men on their deathbeds. RL, however, was not a "special case;" in fact, great pains were taken to select an "ordinary" person for this study. As it turned out, RL was a Southern woman of humble background who was deprived not only of higher education but of health and security most of her life. Yet in the face of five months of grave illness she was able to maintain a general stability of psychological functioning.

The results of this investigation did provide fairly clear evidence of both physiological and psychological decline as a consequence of incurable terminal illness, evidence which certainly outweighed the suggestions of psychological growth apparent in the data. However, the objective signs of the stability of needs inherent in the data carry an important message not to be overlooked. The dying person is still a human being with the capacity to express the entire range of human needs. The medical focus upon the physiological needs is necessary, but far from sufficient, if the individual is to maintain some sense of identity and integrity. Alleviation of physical pain is only one aspect of the situation; the frustration of love and esteem can be equally painful.

The capacity to withstand or even grow under conditions of extreme physical stress, or, perhaps, because of such conditions, is most relevant to our own era…

References

Kübler-Ross, E. (1969). *On death and dying*. New York, NY: Macmillan Publishing Co.

Zinker, J. (1966). *Rosa Lee: Motivation and the crisis of dying*. Painesville, OH: Lake Erie College Press.

POEM

God tricked us.
He made us [fall in] love and
He gave us DEATH -
It is easy to accept death
when you don't love --
But when you love, the beloved's dying is

an outrageous tearing of your heart and soul -
And you are left

screaming into
the empty wilderness...

J.Z., 4/6/98

thirty eight
year old
patient
-AIDS-
African
1998

We Come To Each Other...

After the wars, the
injuries of life,
We come to each other.

After the near-deaths and
        real deaths ---
After having betrayed or
having been betrayed,
We come to each other...

After the solitude, the
loneliness, the
profound grief,
After the lost nights,
the tears, the
accomplishments,
the books,
the skills acquired,
We come to each other
        to rest
        to heal
        to laugh
        to savour life
        fully and just for a moment...
        to be
                free of pain.

J.Z., 4/6/98

1976

11

Entitlement: A Meditation for the Psychotherapy Client

1985

(To be read aloud to oneself)

ENTITLE:
"to give a right or claim to... to empower"
Winston Dictionary;

"... to name, to designate"
Merriam-Webster Dictionary,

"Someone must come along sometime in our lives and tell us, as a witness to a great event might do, "Yes, yes, you are here and yes, you are entitled to be here fully"

Anonymous

Introduction

This little article started as an effort to make a "prayer" or meditation for several of my patients; a kind of homework to be read once or twice a month. I wanted to create a vehicle the use of which would remind them of their entitlements, rights, and privileges that they seem to forget or remain blinded to in spite of months and months of psychotherapy efforts.

I. The World and My Beloved

If I am lucky, I have at least one person in the world who cares about me. This person can be my parent, a child, spouse, teacher, student, friend, companion, work partner, neighbor, or my therapist. This person need not be my lover but I think of him or her as my "beloved."

I deserve to be loved by someone who is important to me, whom I respect and value. I deserve to be cared about.

My beloved is here for me. My beloved is not just a person, but a message, a metaphor of the world. My beloved is the world. What I see in him or her, I can also see in the forest, in flowers, in animals, in all the people, in friends. My beloved opens my eyes and helps me see the world.

Because of this experience, I know that I deserve to see, feel, and ex-press myself in relation to the world in the same way that I see and feel with her or him. My friend takes my hand and takes me into the world. I can see its fullness, its beauty, its dangers, its cruelty, its ugliness, because I can see these things in her or him.

My beloved takes my hand, saying, "This is your world, see and do with it what you see and do with me." My beloved has a crystal-clear message for me: "You are whole, good, kind, strong, imaginative, and you are a world citizen... you belong here . . . this is yours, this is your world..."

II. Nature

I have a responsibility to nature because I have a relationship with it. Nature deserves my care, my protection, and my respect. And nature is there for me. The sky and the moon and the earth and the trees and the flowers and the waters are there for me.

I deserve to fully enjoy everything living (and not living) around me. I can put my feet into the cool pond and I can let the sun shine on my face because I deserve to enjoy these phenomena--I am nature. Nature and I are one (just as my beloved and I are one). Therefore, it is perfectly natural for me to travel, to fly, to swim, to hike, to walk and run, to pick flowers, to play in the rain, to speak to everything that interests me and heightens my energy.

I am on good terms with nature--my own nature and nature of the world outside me. I please nature when I live a full, happy life; and nature is there to support me. The streets and houses are there for me, the shaded alleys are there for me, the wind and snow are there for me, the puddles and animals are there for me, the crickets and birds are there for me, all the pretty and ordinary sounds are there for me (and I am allowed to make pretty and ordinary sounds with pleasure). Even the vacant lots are mine, the roads and bridges are mine, the canals and pleasure boats are mine, the banks and police are mine--they are there to take care of me, to lubricate the freedom of movement I have in the world.

I deserve to enjoy nature. I am nature. I deserve to express my nature out there in the world.

III. People

I am one of millions. But I am as no one else is. I am unique. Like any other person in this world, I am here part-time. And during this time I will show respect to those who show me their respect--and I will avoid people who are disrespectful and poisonous to me. Because I deserve to be happy among people, I like pleasing and taking care of others and I deserve to be pleased and taken care of by others. Just as I am there for (and with) others, they, in turn, are there for me.

People "belong" to me and I to them, in the sense that we all share this world equally. I am not bigger than others, nor are they bigger than I am. I deserve to be loved and cherished, to be seen, to be appreciated, to be praised, to be touched, to be hugged and kissed. People are mine. People are good for me (mostly). They give me what I ask for and want. They will attend to me because I show my right to be attended to. I deserve to be shown respect. I deserve to be given work, food, money, because I am a contributor to people and to the world.

People walk in the streets. It is sunny. And they are beautiful.

They are pleased to see me and they smile at me. Women smile and say hello, with pleasure, to me. Children love me and men greet me with pleasure. People behold me with pleasure. I can ask for anything from people because I am lovely and good and kind, and I deserve to partake of their generosity and love. I deserve to do anything I please. I belong here. I belong with people. I can go anywhere and do anything I please, as long as I am not mean or destructive to others. I belong to the social fabric of this world and I am happy being among people. People will often go out of their way to please me. Why? Because I am me and I deserve to be pleased... and because I repeatedly please others.

IV. Work

I deserve to do the work that turns me on! I am a worker. I love my work. How do I know that my work is not just my "job?" Because my work and I are friends. Because my work stimulates my curiosity and my energy. Because I work with people. My work and I are one, just as my beloved and I are one. I don't separate "work" from "pleasure." My work is one form of pleasure because I express all of me in my work. My work is one of my thrusts in life. It gives me direction. I organize much of my life around my work. Work is growth for me!

As I grow, mature, learn, read, go to the movies, travel--as I do all these things--my work gets better and richer and more skillful and elegant. I give my heart and soul to my work, and people are pleased with what I create. My presence enhances people and helps them become more of who they are. My presence makes people feel affirmed, whole, good, "right" on the inside. And their presence affirms me.

Employers are pleased to pay me for my work. It is only one limited way they can show their gratitude for my giving. I deserve to be paid, to have all the money I need to take care of myself and my family. I deserve to earn a good living.

I deserve to use my money any way I please: to take care of my house, to travel, to buy presents for myself and others. I deserve to live well and fully. I have earned this right with my struggling, my reading, my experiences, my education, and my work. I need not falsely humble my accomplishments to others. I need not render myself smaller than I am or bigger than I really feel to gain the respect of others. I simply need to show myself, to make myself visible.

As a worker, a friend, a member of a group or family, as a person who makes myself known and seen in the world, I deserve to live my life fully, with pleasure, and to pass the pleasure on to others.

V. Relatives

Oh, relatives, they are so problematical. They--our mothers and fathers--created us and loved us the best way they knew how. Parents can't please us. Parents, brothers, sisters, and cousins are human beings! They are not fully qualified (nor should they be) to "make us happy" and to fulfill all our needs. They can't. Sometimes parents--mostly out of their own hunger and bitterness--can hurt us deeply. And we hurt them as well! Sometimes parents can damage us irreparably. And no one can give us back our early purity and innocence. No one can fully re-parent us. But we long to go back to our parents, our roots, over and over again to be loved and affirmed, to be praised and to be held--to be told we are "good," we are "gifted," and we are "special."

I must learn to take the best of my parents and to spit out the parts that don't fit or that hurt me. I must learn to have boundaries and to have my own identity and not to depend on my parents to affirm me.

Relatives are people. Some people can give and others just want to take, to sap us of our good nature, of our vitality. Some people get pleasure from praising us, while others prefer to "make" us feel obligated and to "make" us feel guilty. So is the world. And the world of our parents is the same world. But we don't have to swallow what others give us.

We must learn to be separate to affirm our own goodness and wholeness. I deserve to be loved, and if my parents or my family can't give me affirmation, I can move into the vast world of people and help myself to what is there for me, what is possible, what is offered.

For the most part, the world of people is good. People have pleasure giving and when I take from them (that which didn't come from family), I give others satisfaction. The more people give to me, the more generous I feel toward them. It is in this repeated bridging of give and take that trust, respect, and caring become real to me.

I will be compassionate toward my parents. In loving myself fully, I will learn to forgive my parents for hurting me. In forgiving them, I will indirectly demonstrate that, in spite of their faults, they created a sweet, kind, good child: a whole human being. My parents succeeded after all. They helped create a person who is capable of compassion and forgiving--a person who is whole, a person who feels fully embedded in the world, a person who can give to others, and a person who can take the gifts of others and savor them.

I deserve to have a sense of resolution and peace about my parents. I deserve to move on--and in my own generation, to struggle with the dilemmas of doing a fine job, caring for, parenting, and mentoring others.

VI. On Being a Victim

Because I have experienced so few breaks in my life, I feel like a victim. I feel as if the world won't cooperate in my struggle to become myself. I often feel mired in the goo of daily difficulties--as if people and circumstances are dragging me down. I feel victimized. But as I live on and grow and begin to see the light of day in psychotherapy, the very label of victim becomes an encumbrance to me. I am tempted to blame others for my own lack of energy and inner push. Self-righteously, I focus on the faults of others. When well-meaning friends try to help me and don't hit the mark, I am tempted to feel victorious over their "incompetence": no one can do "right" for me. I render my friends and family (and, at times, my therapist) helpless when I tell them that they don't understand and have never lived the sort of pain I have experienced. My pain is a badge that keeps me isolated from loved ones, keeps me feeling special in my suffering.

"If only" has become part of my daily language: "If only my parents had sent me to college." "If only I weren't maligned by my boss." "If only I had more professional opportunities." "If only I was part of the 'inner circle' in my company." "If only I could stop smoking and lose a little weight"... ad infinitum.

I now realize that, over the years, my "If onlys" started as expressions of regret and were slowly raised to the status of shields of protection and slogans of protest against a cruel world. I have run out of regrets. Now I want to live the life that is possible for me, to find what is good enough for me and to live it with some pleasure.

I must learn to shed my badge of pain because I have worn it too long and it no longer serves to protect me as it did many years ago. I am entitled to find the goodness that my pain has served so I can let go of it and move on in my life. I am entitled to take back the power I have projected onto others so that I can use it directly to get what I need and want from the world.

To give up feeling the victim, I may have to live through a period of owning how I can victimize others by rendering them helpless and stupid. Only when I can recognize the aesthetically unpleasant notion of my capacity as a victimizer, will I learn how to carry my power fully, competently, compassionately. Unlike my elders who abused me, I will use my power to engage, to take care of, to love, to teach, and to be intimate--rather than to beat, oppress, and intimidate others. I am entitled to give up my badge of victim and to carry my strength gracefully. I am entitled to walk straight in the streets and to see the world as a place I can influence.

* * *

In caring for my friends, I am able to see the world, to see it in its wholeness, and to be a whole person. In being able to love one person, I can see the lovable parts of all others. I deserve to enjoy life, to participate in and savor nature and people. I deserve to do the work I love and to feel fully involved in my work. I deserve to work as much or as little as I please and to be well rewarded for my efforts. I deserve to be well paid for my work and to use my money in the service of living a full, rich, generous life.

I am glad to have been born, to be alive, and to strive and hope for a better life (for myself, my family, my friends). I have the right to be angry for not having received everything I needed from my parents, but that does not entitle me to hurt others. As I grow and find ways of fulfilling my needs and as my boundaries grow clearer and stronger, I will feel more compassion for others and be able to forgive them. I will strive to see all sides of people's actions, to recognize and struggle with the good and the bad in the world.

1985

Song 1

Follow the melody within

Follow the rhythm directing you forward
Don't hesitate
Don't turn back

Follow your life blood as long as it flows
Don't stop crying
Don't stop wailing

Don't stop moving with your fist clenched tight
Yet follow your melody

And follow your eastward move into the woods
where the living breath awaits you
and where Life is celebrated

Song 2

Fame and Fortune are shit. It is
only love that counts
castles decay
Halls are sterile
Marble turns gray
It is only love that counts

J.Z., 3/11/96

12

In Search of a Therapeutic Eclecticism

1992

An interview by Irving Bailin

Irving Bailin: Joseph, from your background and experiences of different therapists and modalities of therapy, why is it, do you thing, that there is such heated dispute between body-oriented therapists and more verbal or mental therapies.

Joseph Zinker: I feel that people are attracted to different therapies in a sense out of their own pathology. For example, the obsessive-compulsive is attracted to a psychoanalytic approach which will make him or her even more obsessive-compulsive than before. The actor-outer who has blocked sensory life and the sharpness and clarity of personal awareness is going to want to cry and yell and smash pillows and will continue acting out. So, frequently, the therapies are not matched to the needs of individual. Another ingredient that creatures the split is that a therapist becomes converted to a therapy the way one would become converted to a religion and does not examine his or her needs as a total human being--or the needs of patients or friends. The psychoanalyst creates more obsessionals who are able to talk in greater and better detail about their phobias and stay phobic. The pillow-pounders and screamers are able to act on their impulses much more powerfully. But often they report a kind of homogenized peacefulness which lacks the detail of good, crisp awareness.

Irving: This is almost an answer to the general question I planned to ask: Do the verbal and the body therapies deal with the same problems, personality types, and/or growth issues; or are they dealing with different kinds of problems? Furthermore, do the patient or the method select each other, and are the outcomes therefore quite different for the different forms of therapy we are dealing with here? By verbal therapies, I mean to include psychoanalysis, client-centered, group therapies, cognitive, and rationally motivated therapies. Under body therapies I am including Rolfing, Bio-motivated therapies, and all the Reichian forms.

Joseph: There is no question in my mind that they address themselves to different issues and persons, but we have to be careful because there are different levels of sophistication. You and I are sophisticated enough to know that if after two years of psychoanalysis, we still have a stiff neck, we may need to integrate that with Gestalt and maybe Bioenergetic work. For the most part, the patient in the street hears about Irv or Joseph being a "good therapist" and comes in with only a vague idea about the method we use. In that case, the therapy most often is a method applied to every patient rather than fitting the method to the problem. I see this as the biggest problem our profession engenders: we tend to put a template on everybody--whether the person is a criminal, a neurotic, a psychopath, an arsonist who cannot love and touch another person's life, or whatever. We do the same routine that we have perfected on everybody we see.

Irving: We have had a lot of heat around these problems with very little light.

Joseph: My sense is that we need a theoretically elegant therapeutic eclecticism which would integrate a number of therapies in terms of the levels needed to reach a given person, taking into account both the development of the person and the way in which he or she actually functions from day to day. If we had such a theory, then we could have a whole diagnostic method by which to say, "Well, Irv has already reached a certain level of awareness, but his muscles are lazy; they are not as bright as his awareness." In fact, Wilhelm Reich pointed out that you have to do two kinds of analysis: the psychoanalysis in which you handle all the conflicts, and then the body therapy to get rid of the character armor that supported the neurosis in the first place.

Irving: Kind of a total developmental overview?

Joseph: Right. Even 30 years ago, Wilhelm Reich was already moving in that direction and then the whole thing disappeared when he died. I can give you one example of a very simple model in which this operates very beautifully with Gestalt, where you can take that model and plug in a different therapy depending on where the person is functioning at any given time in his or her life and where he or she is stuck at any given level of psychological functioning.

Irving: You say you already have that model?

Joseph: Sure, I wrote it up in my book, *Creative Process in Gestalt Therapy* (1977). For short, it is the Awareness-Excitement-Contact Continuum developed at the Gestalt Institute in Cleveland. Very briefly, it has to do with moving from sensation to awareness to mobilization of energy to action to contact to completion to withdrawal and once again into sensation. My theory is that you can take these various therapies and fit them into various functions within the cycle of the person.

Irving: That sounds fascinating.

Joseph: For example: Rolfing and Bioenergetics and Primary Therapy work at the level of mobilization of energy and action and contact. They do the least work in the area of awareness and withdrawal. To work on withdrawal you have to go to a Guru from India and learn meditation. That is one therapy you did not include. Why is it we are neglecting that? Is it because we are an action-oriented society? Here everything is action. You have to do something to make something happen! Now psychoanalysis neglects excitement, mobilization of energy systems, action systems, and focuses on different levels of awareness. You learn how you are aware, how to scoop up repressions and fully understand them. It does not guarantee in any way that you will change your action systems.

Irving: It is like the experience I have as an unsophisticated musician. I play the guitar and sing. I play by ear. I have no musical training. Often I hear nuances very clearly in particular songs or voices, but I can't reproduce them. It's terribly frustrating.

Joseph: That's a beautiful example. It's like you have an awareness and some sensation, but you have difficulty bridging your awareness and your sensation with some sort of skeletal-muscular activity.

Irving: Yes, I'm missing the "means-whereby."

Joseph: Exactly. And the very best psychoanalyst will not be able to help you however long and hard you work. Now the very simple model I'm proposing may not be able to answer all the requirements of a therapist, but if you use the cycle you will find, for example, if you are dealing with a criminal then you need to move into a cycle not from awareness to expression, but just the other way around: from expression to awareness. You don't need to teach criminals to breathe and scream. They can breathe and scream and kill ten people. You need to send them for psychoanalysis so they understand how their behavior is ruining their lives. If you have a plain, ordinary psychotherapist who is an obsessional like you and me, what he or she needs is not more awareness but to be able to tell someone to get lost and to really modify behavior in the direction of freedom of expression which the already clear awareness dictates.

Irving: What you are saying reminds me of when I first conceived the idea for this issue of *Voices*. I was with Bob and Mary Goulding at the Quebec American Academy of Psychotherapists Summer Workshop a couple of years ago and I shared a fantasy with them. My fantasy was that I was God--if you will remember, in fact, it was in your workshop that we had an ex-minister who was giving advice, rescuing everyone, and no one could make any contact with him, and I had the fantasy that he should play God and make a world of his own out of us and the universe-room we were occupying. Remember?

Joseph: Sure.

Irving: So in my fantasy in Quebec, I decided to play God and I came down on earth and scooped everybody up out of analysts' chairs and couches and took them over and dumped them into this big circus where there were Rolfers and Bioenergetics and Yogas, Aikido's, Tai Chi's and all kinds of even crazier "meshugaas" going on. Then I scooped everybody who was already there in that circus and dumped them into analysts' and client-centered offices, clapping my hands and proclaimed that I had solved all the problems of the world. The fantasy came from watching and listening to the defenses of therapists in the workshop.

Joseph: That would be an act of charity and wisdom. The analysts need to breathe, move, dance; and the body folks need cognitive depth, clarity, and crispness. I had an interesting experience with a Rolfer. I swear to you, he didn't take five minutes to ask me anything about my medical history, my work, family life, nothing! He looked at my body and said I had the chest of a five year old, and went to work on me. He would make me groan, but I had the clear sense that he did not care about me as a person. He had only the respect for my body as a machine that needed correcting. But that is another issue having to do with the training of therapists!

Irving: It does point up the issue that you started with thought, that I would translate as, the patient tends to select the therapist who is congruent with his or her defense system so there is a mismatch in terms of the patient's needs.

Joseph: Yes, there is no question about it. I have had a number of patients with histories of being schizoid, scattered, unable to focus, unable to ground themselves, who go into expression therapies. So you have the hysteric who needs to learn to focus going into Bioenergetics. It is crazy. I'm sure you can think of examples of really borderline people, very scattered in their awareness, doing work which just makes them more scattered.

Irving: Joseph, I'm remembering a girl, very unfocused, in a workshop of yours six years ago. I remember the piece of work you did with her. You had her sit with her eyes closed and imagine that in her lap was a bowl of magic liquid. She was to dip her hands into the liquid in slow motion, bring the liquid to her face, and then very slowly wash her face with this magic potion that would awaken her.

Joseph: That's beautiful, but I have no memory of that.

Irving: I still remember it and the magic transformation that came over her afterwards.

Joseph: I slowed her down. I am discovering a whole syndrome in people who are not grounded, the so-called hysteric, people who are not grounded in several basic ways. First of all, they speak very quickly like I'm doing right now because they are so excited. Secondly, they hear voices in their heads which are competing--I don't mean psychotic hallucinations, I mean there is a lot of noise--static--in their heads. Thirdly, they don't experience the gravity in their bodies so they are always pulling up their shoulders, and their asses don't fully rest in whatever they're in. Before anyone can do any kind of work, awareness work, sensation work, movement work, they have to start with this base. A psychoanalyst or client-centered therapist has to realize that before a patient can fully hear him or her, the patient has to be grounded in those three ways. Of course, before the therapist can hear the patient, he or she also must be grounded in those three ways. The moment the therapist gets stuck on content, listens only to the meanings, he or she is defeated.

Irving: Because he or she has ignored process. Yes. Joseph, what are some of the diagnostic indications for different forms of therapy? Who would you see as appropriate for specific methods like Rolfing and Bioenergetics and Gestalt or what-have-you? In our previous conversation, I mentioned to you that I found it difficult to work in a Gestalt framework with narcissistic personality disturbances. Because of their exhibitionism, that is all they seemed to get out of their work, or else they were so frightened and vulnerable about exhibiting themselves that they could not get into it.

Joseph: It is difficult for me to translate classical psychiatric nomenclature into what we are doing phenomenologically. If, for example, you take someone who is high on a schizoid scale, what does that mean? It means that that person is not able to own his or her experience and understand its details. That means they need to bridge their sensation with their awareness. What kind of therapy does that problem require? It is a therapy that pays attention to your experience and not to my assumptions. That therapy could be psychoanalytic if it pays attention to sensation and not just words. It's certainly Gestalt. Rolfing? I don't see any Rolfers doing that at all. The Primal folks are dealing with much bigger pieces than that and my experience tells me such large pieces are indigestible; they cannot usually be integrated into the personality after the work is finished. The original Reichians might get into that. It depends on the sensitivity and personal development of the individual therapist. I don't know about the newer Reichians. To diagnose the schizophrenic or the schizoid condition phenomenologically means to say, "here is where we need to do the bridging." What we need is to teach persons to see and then connect the scene with their thinking and feeling. It is really not so simple. It is a complex diagnostic and methodological task.

Irving: You're evoking some powerful imagery in me. You mentioned schizophrenics and I'm thinking also of borderline psychoses. Can you say more about the psychoses and dealing with them appropriately?

Joseph: Once again, it has to do with the linking-up. I think what the psychotic does is jump from the sensation to misinterpreted awareness to action which may not relate to the original sensory experience.

Irving: Like a little child?

Joseph: Perhaps like a very frightened child. If I were psychotic, I would look into your eyes and then maybe "see" you examining my arms and then jump to the active mode of seeing you mutilate me. I might run before you got me.

Irving: Are you saying in effect that the therapist has to supply the awareness rather than rely on the patient to produce it?

Joseph: Well, certainly with psychotics I wouldn't start by getting into their fantasies of how they are going to be decapitated or de-balled or whatever. That will only frighten them. They will have to do much smaller pieces of work on sensation. Gestalt has a tendency among many of us to be sweeping, broad, and bold. That level of excitement is frightening to psychotics. You have to keep them going back from sensation to awareness and again to sensation and awareness while paying attention to excitement. They must learn to identify the actual sensory roots of ideation. It boils down to how much excitement that person can tolerate before breaking and starting to flip out and "act out."

Irving: Joseph, you have had a long experience in psychotherapy now-20 years. Let's go back. Do you see any change in prevailing pathologies between then and now?

Joseph: Sure. I see more people who are narcissistic, who do not have a sense of community.

Irving: Do you agree with the criticism that Gestalt has encouraged this?

Joseph: For the main part, I do. Especially the West Coast branch of Gestalt. I think that Fritz Perls was deeply misunderstood. You have to remember that he came out of a Victorian background in which he just naturally assumed some things about being a "mensch." We saw Fritz trying to break out of his own authoritarian mold. He was learning to ask for what he wanted out of a very rich apperceptive mass, of having done a great deal of service for others for 50 years. For him it was a very important transition in life. But when he encouraged young people to "wipe their own asses" and gave them "I am I and you are you and if it happens between us it's nice, and if not it is too bad," he stimulated the "ME" revolution. So a whole generation of young people picked up these slogans and made caricatures of themselves with "I don't give a shit about what you think. This is what I want." For these children who never learned how to give, to keep wiping their own asses became a very lonely place. They were forlorn, hardened, and unattached. In marriage or living together, they didn't know how to give to and take care of the other person. They would insist on getting their own way. They would have to negotiate or argue about whether to go to a movie or not because they did not know how to compromise or to please the other out of love and graciousness and caring.

Irving: It sounds like you're saying that in the last 20 years we have lost sight of what was really good and beautiful about the "Jewish Mother" and the capacity to take pleasure in giving and caring for another.

Joseph: Yes, and we have also maligned religion. Even though religion deserved it for not updating its rituals to fit our spiritual needs and our existential pain, we ended up throwing out the baby with the bath water.

Irving: Joseph, you have taken exception to the "I-focus" in Gestalt. Are you also critical of the contemporary trend to "Me-as-body" in psychotherapy, analogous to Jung's criticism of Freud's preoccupation with sex in psychoanalysis?

Joseph: You know, I really believe in Freud's assumptions about libidinal energy, that the most profound inspirations grow out of sexual longings. I did very simple experiments with my painting. I found that when I didn't have intercourse for three weeks, I painted beautifully. The moment I had sexual relief my painting deteriorated. I did not have as much energy in it. We have to accept the fact that much of our creative energy grows out of the juices and chemistry inside us. But we cannot fixate at that level. For psychotherapy--for psychotherapists--to grow and develop, we need to grow at every level. We cannot simply learn how to be good listeners or how to be good body appreciators or how to move gracefully. We also have to learn the need for a sense of community, to be "plugged into" something outside ourselves. We need to learn the longing of the human spirit for transcendence. Carl Jung understood this, and he was no eunuch. He used to leave his wife alone, walk down several blocks to his mistress and screw his head off. He understood about having pleasure, but he was also a spiritual man.

Irving: That's a dimension of Jung I never knew about. I did know about his spiritual side.

Joseph: Obviously, if you have a rich life, you can appreciate that ascended dimension in humankind. To make our actions clear and strong requires the capacity to withdraw, to evaluate, to meditate, to think about how we have created the lives we have. If we can pursue those parts of ourselves and integrate them with the Rolfings and the Primal screams and the group therapies and behavior modifications, then we can become whole persons teaching others to become whole persons. We need to keep integrating our meditative mysterious side with our bold actions.

Irving: So what I'm hearing you say is that true spirituality as feeling and awareness has to emerge out of the awareness of real needs and experience of our bodies. And this brings me to another problematic question out of my experience as a therapist. As I get more into body work, I find often as I am cueing in on the other's communication to me, I suddenly become aware of a twistedness in my stomach, for example, or a sharp pain in the back of my neck. I will ask the person what is going on in their body and they will tell me the exact thing that I am experiencing. I have found this also with a number of therapists I have talked to.

Joseph: This is true for me too.

Irving: So how do you deal with this, Joseph?

Joseph: The same way that you deal with it. If I am in contact with a person, my body will mimic their stuckness over and over again. I will ask them to breathe, if I find myself short of breath, or take a deep breath for myself if they can't. That is the beauty of contact. It means that you are really in contact and aware of what is happening.

Irving: Sometimes I go home overwhelmed by these sensations. I have to go out and run three miles or find something else to get myself out of these places. I'm curious to know how others deal with that problem in themselves.

Joseph: There are different ways of doing it. One thing that I do is to move. I use movement in my work. If I begin to feel a pain in my neck, I won't look at the patient. I start working on my neck. Or maybe I get up and pace and ask my patient to pace with me in the office while talking. I try to put my tension to work and cash in on whatever I'm asking the patient to do. Just mimic the patient and join the patient in their new behavior. It's very enlivening.

Irving: So you're saying that you are going to refuse to let the patient give you something that you don't want.

Joseph: I don't want to take it home. I know very clearly the times I do, because I'm exhausted. I literally drag myself to my car. And this brings me to another dimension that is missing from this issue of verbal vs. body therapies: the dimension of systems. Let us say that you are seeing somebody who complains about not being sensitive to other people and you are able to tune in on their problem of seeing you as a person and how that is reflected in their body. Let's say that you have that integrated as a therapy. The problem still remains, how do they operate in this system with you and also how do they operate in the dyadic system with a significant other? I think this is the third piece we must tackle if we want to be holistic. No individual functions in a vacuum. Chances are this person has a contract with a significant other to remain insensitive. If you don't tap into that system and teach them--which analysts never do, by the way--how to break the system agreement for maintaining that insensitivity, you will not create lasting change.

Irving: What you are saying, then, is that the character attitude of a person is in some way supported by a social-psychological system and that system has to be dealt with by them in some behavioral way in order to modify their character attitude.

Joseph: Right. I will give you a very simple example, of projection. You come to me, and look at me and you say to me, "Joseph, you are stingy." Being a Gestalt therapist, I have you explore your own stinginess. Then I look at your body and I say, "Let's work on your body being more expansive." So far, so good. You achieve awareness of the linkage between thinking and feeling in your body. But you come back and you are still projecting. So then I say to you, "Bring your wife." Then what I discover is that your wife does not talk, does not tell you how she really feels and how angry she is. She creates an information vacuum into which you are forced to project. My feeling is that the social-system dimension is very important to add to the other two that we are discussing. My prediction is that individual therapy will be used only in very special cases in the future. It will be the least common form of therapy.

Irving: Are you saying in effect that therapy of the social system and body therapy are going to be…

Joseph: Hopefully, they will become integrated. My fantasy is, if you have a husband with a puffed-up chest, chances are that you'll find a wife with a collapsed chest. If you have a guy who projects and does not see, then you have a wife who does something with her vision or something with her body or with her movement so that she is not seeing.

Irving: There is a Bioenergetic therapist here in Chicago, Bernie Liebowitz, who prefers working with couples because he finds this same dimension of a bioenergetic fitting in relationships.

Joseph: He is already in the forefront of where I think we are going. Why pluck people out of the social system in which they actually function, do a beautiful piece of work, and then let it go down the drain when they go home?

Irving: So, in effect, what you are saying is, whatever that body is that we are working with, that body is nevertheless supported in a medium and the medium must be looked at, not just the body manipulated.

Joseph: Exactly. I couldn't say it any better!

Irving: Excellent, Joseph. I think this has personally been a very productive interview, and is very valuable in terms of the questions that we are trying to confront in this issue of Voices. Can you think of anything that we may have overlooked?

Joseph: I think that the more we become aware of and work with the systems in which people actually function--coupling and family--the more we will reinforce the notion of the richness of community life and the less we will feel isolated as human beings. It is very clear to me that the "me" generation is on the way out. I'm very hopeful that the whole emphasis on "me" and "my needs" and "my growth" and isolation is going to die out because we cannot survive in a "me" world.

A life lived
is a nightmare in daylight.
Every incision of pleasure
bleeds into one's
eyes.
Caught in the slim,
daily corridors of
comfort,
is the space of sudden
asphyxiation -
Laughter mingles ecstasy
with piercing
wildness ...
Then silence.
What is one to do
but to live it out?

J.Z., London, 2/20/00

Dr. Farmer's
Patient, Haiti—
JZ

13

Discussions with the Masters

1990

Interview by Robert L. Harman, Ed.D.

Robert Harman: I just want to have you start talking about whatever emerges for you in thinking about Gestalt therapy theory. Do you have any early thoughts?

Joseph Zinker: I'll begin by saying a few things about awareness and contact, because you had written and asked me to mention those two concepts. With respect to awareness, this is a broad and enormous area. It includes memories, reveries, plans, anticipations, hopes, values, and regrets. Memories have to do with all of the cortical functions and feelings attached to them. In the context of Gestalt theory, we think about awareness as the experience of searching for a figure in a field of randomness and a process of finding the figure out of randomness.

Robert: Could you say more about searching for the figure? Can you give examples?

Joseph: Yes. For example, we sat down and just started cold. You gave me an opportunity to say something. I quickly searched for a way in which I could anchor my beginning. I visualized your letter and the two words that I had underlined in it; so I found a figure--the figure was your letter. Then, I began to develop that figure.

Robert: I understand. This part of the awareness you're talking about has to do with all the cortical functions and cognitions in general--the thinking, planning, feeling, and so on.

Joseph: As I said, awareness is huge. It's like asking, "What is a person?" "What is the meaning of life?" It feels that huge. It includes our ground--the ground out of which we come--so it includes memories and learnings. It's like visualizing the cortex, seeing it in front of me. I remember what the frontal area does. It's all the things I learned in school that interested me and that I kept. All of the ground that is behind me affects what I write, what I say to you at this moment. It's compressed and supporting me and what I'm developing right now with you.

Robert: It's "supporting you" for our contact at this moment?

Joseph: Right! It's supporting me for my contact with myself. That is my own differentiated awareness of what I know. My dialogue between that which I utter and I know. That's one level of contact. Then, building for and preparing for a meaningful contact with you is another level. So there are always at least two levels of contact: one's contact with one's self and one's contact with another. It's impossible sometimes to separate these, though it's important to separate them. It's important to have boundaries.

Robert: I like your description of awareness. It seems different and broader and more encompassing than other Gestalt therapists would define it. I think you're more in tune with my own thoughts about awareness as being support, ground, and huge. When I think of Gestalt theory, awareness is the first thing I think about. I have been interested in it, but not everyone is. Joel Latner said something like, "Well, awareness is important; what more can I say?" That was about all he wanted to say about it.

Joseph: I was a college professor and I used to teach psychology, so those are important concepts to me, not only Gestalt concepts, but as historical ideas in psychology and psychoanalysis. We could spend hours talking about awareness.

Robert: We could probably spend two days talking about it. I think Perls used to say, "In Gestalt therapy, awareness in and of itself can be curative' " He also made some statements that seem kind of ridiculous as I think about it now, but if you asked the patient, "What are you aware of now?" and focused on that, that was Gestalt therapy. That seems rather surface to me now.

Joseph: It's narrow. I think what he was trying to say, what he was trying to emphasize, was that Gestalt therapy deals with awareness and it deals with the present moment--the unfolding. I think he probably copied from Freud. Freud felt that psychotherapy, in order for anything to be psychoanalysis, had to do with awareness and with resistance to awareness. So Freud also had a kind of minimalistic definition of psychoanalysis at some point.

Robert: You mentioned that you need awareness in order to be here with me and so that we can have this contact we're having. After you have contact with your thoughts and memories and you visualize my letter, we may meet at the contact boundary. Could you say more about that meeting and what that means to you?

Joseph: Awareness is a process, and contact is also a process. Again, driving here, I was thinking about what I wanted to say about contact. In the broadest sense, contact is the process by which I get what I want--the process of coming home. I thought about coming home--the process of ultimately getting something that one hopes for. It's the process of feeling fully engaged in a differentiated way with parts of oneself or parts of the other. So, contact is a sweet thing--even if it has to do with conflict. Contact doesn't have to be a good experience; it can be an awful experience. If you and I begin to fight and our boundaries, fully energized, connect, that's contact. Some people think that contact is a touchy-feely business or that it's a good experience in that it's pleasant. Contact doesn't have to be good or pleasant. It's a strong experience of touching either one another psychologically or being touched within oneself.

Robert: You said, "Contact gets me what I need." Here's how I'm connecting that with awareness: you have to be aware of that need first, to have enough aggression or energy, to expend that energy, to get what you need. Does that make sense in what you're thinking?

Joseph: Yes. We can get into the whole question of "If the tree falls in the forest with nobody there to hear it, can we still consider that it made a sound?" in terms of awareness. Even when one isn't aware that one gets what one wants, it still "makes a sound." Contact has still taken place. It is a difficult question to answer; but, in our view, it has to be an aware sense of homecoming rather than an unaware sense. If you're not aware, how do you know whether you're home or somewhere else?

Robert: When we think about contact problems, most of us have various terms for describing it. Sometimes we call it a disturbance at the boundary. I think Miriam Polster's latest description is "self-regulation" at the boundary. But, somehow, our conception is that we do something that interferes with the potential for contact, interferes with or interrupts the actual contact. What are your ideas about that?

Joseph: About interference? Well, there are the usual forms of interference that all of us know about, like deflection. But it's tricky because, while it may be deflection, it's also a way of building that contact between us out of little things which, in the end, can contribute to the richness of our awareness and, therefore, our potential contact. So, I don't put self-regulation into contact. I believe that the self-regulation takes place throughout awareness, excitement, and the contact-withdrawal cycle. Self-regulation is there all the time so that we regulate sensation--how much sensation we let in before the awareness is even formed, so that we don't get overwhelmed. We regulate awareness, of course. We also regulate other people's awareness by distorting or leaving out things, or by lying, or so that we can regulate the level of intimacy. If I were sitting here with some guy from your university whom I had never met, you could be sure I couldn't talk as easily to him and might not reveal as much about myself. So, self-regulation takes place there, and it takes place at the level of mobilization of energy. Retroflection is a very powerful and common form of self-regulation.

Robert: You almost made a face when you said "retroflection."

Joseph: Well, retroflection is exciting. Without it we couldn't have a civilized world. It's a very powerful idea.

Robert: Retroflection is the turning back in or holding in. I think that sometimes, without it, I couldn't have a decent marriage. If one of us didn't retroflect at times, we would have chaos in the relationship.

Joseph: That's right. So, even at the level of awareness, there is retroflection. That is, when you make your sentence shorter, leave out words, or when you do any kind of editing of your language as it comes out of you, you are retroflecting the language. So, retroflection does not have to be skeletal. It can be cortical--a kind of cortical pinching.

Robert: In your book, you mentioned the cycle that most people in Gestalt circles would identify with you. I'm wondering if that's mostly a Joseph Zinker model, or is that a Cleveland model?

Joseph: Actually, I asked around and, by the time I wrote the book, it was the Cleveland model. Then I asked how that model was formed. Well, as you know in Perls' book, Gestalt Therapy, as well as in his previous book, *Ego, Hunger and Aggression*, he talks about excitement. He talks about awareness. He talks about energy. He talks about the figure. He doesn't talk about awareness, but he talks about bright formation of a really brilliant figure, a clearly differentiated figure. But he talks about those concepts as if they were satellites in the sky--which, in some ways, is really more real. Having asked around at the Gestalt Institute of Cleveland, I was told that Miriam Polster and Bill Warner (Bill is now deceased) originally put it together in some talk during a faculty meeting. They put together that particular order of those phenomena and, therefore, made a kind of phenomenological model of the progression of these events. I think it's an arbitrary model. It helps to think of mobilization of energy as coming just before action. What it leaves out is that you need mobilization of energy before a clear figure is formed at the awareness level. The energy at the cortical level required is very tiny as opposed to energy to do an experiment with your body or the energy it takes to burst out in anger, both of which are huge. So, it's artificial in the sense that, at every level, we have energy. And, at every level, we have awareness--and so on. But it's a nice little model and we like it.

Robert: Well, I think it is arbitrary, as most models are, when you're trying to describe something--that is a human happening. I don't know any other way of doing it, except by attaching some arbitrary labels to the events that we think are there.

Joseph: But it's clearly a Cleveland Gestalt Institute model. I think you may want to ask around more, but I think it was started originally by those two people in an informal chat and discussion. I'm pretty certain I was the first person to write it up and publish it.

Robert: Yes, I think so. That's the first place I recall seeing it. I'm thinking about the first time I came across anything of yours; Jim Simkin gave us all a copy when we were in training, a copy of that beautiful article titled, "Gestalt Therapy Is Permission to Be Creative." I think it was only about one page in *Voices*. I read that and it kind of zinged me. It felt so good for me to feel like I take what I have, my background, which is rural and country, and earthy, and mobilize that to be a Gestalt therapist. I don't have to introject Jim Simkin or Joseph Zinker, or whomever I'm working with at that time. Reading that article seemed to unburden me.

Joseph: Like a Declaration of Independence?

Robert: Yes, by George, this is what it's all about. I can be me in whatever way is right for me. With some training and theoretical grounding, I can be a Gestalt therapist. I'm not implying that you just do your thing in Gestalt therapy. I thought that was one of the nicest articles about Gestalt therapy I have ever read. What are you writing now?

Joseph: Sonia Nevis and I are busily working the application of Gestalt theory to couples and family therapy. Speaking of the cycle, Sonia helped me think of the cycle as an interactional phenomenon, so we are calling it the interactive cycle. If you visualize the sine curve, we just superimpose a number of idiosyncratic different sine curves so that we can look at how contact takes place between more than two people. We describe that. We have a little article you can buy at the institute which summarizes that notion of interactive cycle. It talks about resistances as interactive phenomena, rather than a single-person phenomenon.

Robert: Could you elaborate a little bit about resistances as interactive phenomena?

Joseph: Yes. Let's take projection. In order for you to project, I have to be mysterious. The moment I tell you, "No, no, Bob, that's not right, this is how I feel..." you can't project. So projection takes place between two people: one who maintains himself as mysterious and the other one who is not willing to ask questions to find out.

Robert: It's almost like an enabler. In alcoholic circles, they would say "enabler."

Joseph: Exactly. Introjection is easy. You need somebody who wants to swallow whole and another person who force-feeds. Retroflection is one person being in discomfort and the other person not inquiring about what the discomfort is about, or what's wrong, so that the first person then has to take care of himself or herself. Both people are stingy.

Robert: Here's an example in a couple: if I'm sulking around the house and pouting over something my wife isn't doing and I don't tell it to her and she doesn't ask, we have the interactive process going on.

Joseph: Right. And the result is a deadness in the system because your sulking deadens you. Also, with that interaction not having taken place, the marriage experiences the deadness.

Robert: If I'm willing to ask her for what I want, we get out of that.

Joseph: If you're willing to ask and if she's willing to listen.

Robert: Yes. But what happens if she's not willing to listen?

Joseph: Then you're both in trouble!

Robert: I'm thinking that if that is an interactive phenomenon, can we undo it if I'm willing to ask, but my wife doesn't want to respond? I know we are in deep trouble.

Joseph: Then you just reverse roles. She's the sulker and you're the sulkee, so the system is still considered retroflective. She's holding back. You need her there. If you follow her around the house and keep badgering her and asking her and she loses her temper and starts yelling at you, you've undone the retroflection. But it takes some energy on your part. You may not have enough energy to bother.

Robert: It's fascinating to think in terms of interaction and how it works out that way. In essence, we keep our resistant system going by our own behaviors.

Joseph: Right. It's the defense mechanism and resistance developed in a two-person system--between mother and child, for example. That's where it started.

Robert: I agree with what you're saying, and I sometimes think that we learn a preferred or a favorite style of interrupting our contact potential in childhood. Retroflection, for example, is carried with us through our years, unless we get good therapy or we pair up with someone who doesn't put up with that and rejects us.

Joseph: Hopefully, we are lucky enough to pair up with someone who doesn't put up with that kind of stuff, one who makes us feel loved at the same time, so that we can afford to practice new behavior and not get too scared.

Robert: In your practice, are you working with many families and couples?

Joseph: Yes.

Robert: Do you see a difference in how you work with the couple as compared to the family?

Joseph: There are many differences. For one thing, you know you have a huge amount of data with a family.

Robert: Right. Where do I go with all this stuff? It can be overwhelming.

Joseph: Also, with a family, I feel more like an animal trainer with a chair. The organism is much larger and, therefore, I have to clearly establish my role as the "Big Dad." Not that I don't do that with couples, but I think the power of who is in charge has to be quite evident with a larger organism.

Robert: Yes, and sometimes that's the battle right there--who's going to be in charge of this therapy that we are here for. The family does all kind of neat tricks to keep us from doing our work.

Joseph: That's right. They do it to keep themselves from being fully in contact with each other. Which, of course, keeps us from doing our work--or it keeps us with our noses to the grindstone, keeps us working, because they keep us looking for how they manage in such an elegant way to interrupt each other or to keep the figure from emerging.

Robert: Joseph, are there any areas that we're not talking about that you think are important?

Joseph: It depends. There are so many things we could talk about.

Robert: I have a few other things I'd like us to talk about. Besides Gestalt psychology and psychoanalysis, do you see some other contributions to our field of Gestalt therapy as being important and worth noting?

Joseph: Jim Kepner has recently written a book on Gestalt phenomenological body therapy. I think the whole area of body phenomenology, body awareness, is very important. Fritz was in therapy with Reich, and he stole a lot of ideas from Reich and simply made them his own. So Reichian, Neo-Reichian, bioenergetic, any kind of body awareness or therapy is very important. In one interview I did for *Voices*, I took the awareness cycle and looked at the various important therapies. We could do that, too. For example, between the axis between sensation and energy and movement is the axis of various body therapies. Then you have the awareness therapies like psychoanalysis and the various cognitive therapies that rely heavily on awareness, cognition, control, and so on. Or you have the various therapies that have to do with withdrawal and sensation. The very beginning part that philosophically deals with the meditation and the far Eastern religious experience, and body sensations, and transpersonal phenomenon, and all of that. I would say that everything matters. Every new theory is worth exploring. Even then, having finished exploring, we are still very limited. We still have to read a lot. We have to be involved with the arts. We have to travel. We should go to the theatre. We should be involved in any human endeavor of a creative nature if we want to be good Gestalt therapists.

Robert: I agree. From what you're saying, I gather that training is never completed, or maybe I should say that learning is never completed. We don't stop when we get a certificate from somewhere. We continue to incorporate into our persona the various experiences we may have, and we continue to grow.

Joseph: Bob, I like to differentiate between training and education. The tradition of training almost always has to do with the technology of a given craft--the theory and methods. I think we turn out a lot of trained people who are not educated. Education is much broader. People may be well trained, but they are not necessarily well-developed human beings, not well-educated.

Robert: As one who trains, I have some difficulty in stimulating people to go beyond training. Many people are interested in the technical aspects only. To me, that's a very narrow focus.

Joseph: I mentioned in my opening speech at the Gestalt Conference that we have a history of a man in his seventies teaching us to drop our heads and go into our sensation. Lose your mind and come to your senses. He could afford to loose his mind. He was seventy and had so much in his mind. A bunch of mindless twenty-year-olds heard that slogan with very little ground. We had contributed to a generation of pretty crazy stuff. Some of it was exciting and helped us loosen up a little bit; but when those words fell on the minds of youngsters who didn't have the awareness and richness of the old man, we produced a lot of imitators who didn't know what the hell they were doing, even though I suppose they were trained in some way. So, we have a history of making trouble and contributing to that unwillingly, because Fritz projected it. He didn't project his own liberation from a Victorian kind of stuffy background of which he had different doctorates. For him it was a liberation. For a young person it was imprisonment to stay with the senses.

Robert: I believe I've heard Jim Simkin say that Fritz Perls founded Gestalt therapy and almost destroyed it. I think Jim was thinking about those kinds of sentences and of people catching on to the narrow surface part that it would bring one to.

Joseph: Yes, that's right. It didn't trouble those of us who came from rich Judeo-Christian backgrounds where, if you read a book, your mother smiled, no matter what you were reading. We did a lot of acting out, like everybody else in the sixties. But, somehow, we were able to plow that back into all the things we learned and make something out of it.

Robert: How are things going with your training? My own experience is that I have fewer people interested in training these days. The phenomenon in Florida is that people who are licensed in all the disciplines have to accrue continuing education hours. So people are asking, "Where can I get the cheapest hours?" The idea of training where one immerses oneself in learning, truly an education whether it's learning a craft or reading, doesn't sell very well. It took me four years in Florida before I was able to get enough people together to do a training group. Now, I have stimulated enough interest by giving speeches and demonstrations and everything I could and, finally, I have enough interest for a training group. However, it's more difficult to interest people in the investment of training and learning about Gestalt therapy than it was in the seventies. Does that fit with your experience?

Joseph: We don't have much of that experience at the institute. I think that we are now entrenched in the world. We have an international reputation, but I think that there are fewer qualified people at the doctoral level. I think that by the time people get a doctorate they are so exhausted and so desensitized that they just want to rest for a dozen years. We do have fewer people. We also have a kind of impatience with depth, witnessed by an interest in the cognitive, an interest in hypnosis, in brief therapies, and so on. I think there is more interest in how to do it quickly, how to take the symptoms away, and less interest in awareness-type therapies. I think that's a disturbing trend. As an awareness-based therapist, it's one thing to acquire various tricks and use them selectively with certain people because they're useful. It's another thing to start there without the kind of ground we appreciate and require. I see fewer people who are, strictly speaking, phenomenologists. Fewer students are interested in learning how to observe behavior. They don't appreciate how beautiful it is. They just want tricks. It's a pity.

Robert: I agree wholeheartedly. That trend is disturbing. Symptom removal seems to be almost the therapy of the day. The depth where one would develop awareness and expand awareness, or even expand contact potential, does not interest a lot of people.

Joseph: Right. It's good to look at the other side of that. There is good reason. If I see someone, I'm thinking about the influence on biological psychiatry. If I see someone week after week and they are depressed and I don't feel like I'm budging them, I don't hesitate to get somebody to prescribe Elavil or some other antidepressant drug. It's a miracle. The drug makes them sleep better, concentrate better, and take care of themselves. Then, it is possible to do therapy with some of these people. So, sometimes, therapy is discouraging. It's difficult work, and most of us may search for shortcuts at times.

Robert: I agree. I have found in the therapy I received that I became very interested in me. I found myself fascinated at times. To think that I could have settled for someone to remove my symptoms would have been cheating for me. For me, therapy was a great discovery experience, confidence-building and all of that.

Joseph: I think, probably, because you were basically well. You could go from one model of wellness to another goal within your wellness, and so on. That's very nice. But some people whom we see are quite sick. That makes it difficult for them to be fascinated with themselves. Their illness interferes.

Robert: They would be the people for whom we might utilize some kind of drug therapy or other therapy to remove the symptoms and then see if they could become fascinated with themselves.

Joseph: Right. I like the Maslowian model very much. You can see that if they are so sick that they are sick at the level of physiological and security needs, we've got to go there first to support them physiologically and that whole basic sphere before they can move into love and belongingness and self-actualization.

Robert: It seems like we've covered a lot of ground. There are some other things that I have some interest in. I was thinking about the book, *Ego, Hunger and Aggression*, which I conceptualize as a forerunner to the development of Gestalt therapy, and then the later book by Perls, Hefferline, and Goodman. Do you see that book as contributing to Gestalt therapy theory?

Joseph: I never took to it, Bob. I read it and re-read it and never got turned on or inspired like I did with *Gestalt Therapy*. *Gestalt Therapy* was my Bible. I read it, re-read it, and still read it. I never went for *Ego, Hunger, and Aggression*. I never credited the book very much with some important things.

Robert: I have had your experience with *Gestalt Therapy*. I've worn out one copy. Because it was important for me to keep, I have rubber bands all around it. I have a dirty copy and a clean copy. I go to that book frequently when I'm stuck with a client or when I'm writing and I feel the need to elaborate. I can usually find something in there to get me unstuck. I must have read it a dozen times and I learn something new each time. There is so much in there.

Joseph: Fritz didn't write well. His writing was dense and you could see that he was translating from German into English all the time. Nevertheless, the density came not just from poor writing, it came out of the density of his background and his awareness.

Robert: People who are not Gestalt therapists have given us a look. They say things like, "There really isn't a theory in Gestalt therapy." We have no theory. One of the things that they base that on is that book isn't easily read. Some say, "There is nothing in that book; it is too dense." The legend has it that Paul Goodman rewrote it in such a fashion that it couldn't be introjected. Some people are turned off by that book.

Joseph: Well, it's not written well.

Robert: Right. I find two things that people tell me about Gestalt therapy that turns them off. One is that book and the other is the *Gloria* tape. That tape terrorizes graduate students. They see the tape and think that's Gestalt therapy. Once in a while, I'll get invited to speak to a class and their instructor will say, "Bob Harman is coming over; he is a Gestalt therapist," and they are prepared for something awful to happen. They think that I will be mean, nasty, abrasive or something other than what I am.

Joseph: Well, those of us who were naive or uneducated, and there are still those around, were scared by Fritz in those early days, unless we knew him. I knew him relatively well, so I wasn't scared, but most people were scared of him. I had a very similar experience watching Carl Whitaker the first time. He seemed like a real mean son of a bitch until I got to know him and understood where he was coming from. So the purpose of psychotherapy is not to entertain or to stroke people's eyes or to put salve on their wounds. And I didn't know that. I thought it was to make people feel good. I didn't know psychotherapy is intended to ask people to get in touch with who they are and what they do, and the pain of that, as well as the pleasure. So these men were right on the edge. They got the person, or the family, or the couple, in touch with what they were actually doing. It wasn't always a pretty sight. To this day, there are Gestalt therapists who imitate only that part of Fritz which worked with mobilizing anxiety and frustration. It's a one-sided kind of therapy. It doesn't have a full range. Some people are drawn to Gestalt therapy because of that and because of sadistic Gestalt therapists.

Robert: Yes, and they attracted those kinds of patients--patients who would put up with that and would accept it. It's unfortunate that we do not have more film and video-tapes available. I reviewed one last summer by John Swanson, who is at the University of Oregon. He did a demonstration. I have been recommending it to people because it is so different than the *Gloria* film. He appears to be mostly interested in how this woman interrupts her own contact process and focuses on that in the therapy. He doesn't do it in any kind of a way that people could interpret as harsh or abrasive. It's good contrast for people to see that after they've seen the *Gloria* film.

Joseph: Sonia Nevis is in the process of producing a tape of Gestalt therapists working with a family. She's working with a professional team. I'm hoping that eventually that tape will be available. Also, she is a permission-giving kind of therapist. I should say an empowering kind of person.

Robert: As you are making that statement, I'm thinking that, in some ways, I feel like we are in our infancy in Gestalt therapy. We are working with families, couples, and there isn't a body of literature yet about Gestalt therapy with families and couples. I have an article coming out shortly in the *International Journal of Family Psychiatry* (Harman, 1986) on working with couples. When I was writing that, I began to look for other things. There is not a lot of material at all. As I talked to people, I say that we do not write about our work with families and couples.

Joseph: That's true. It's very difficult to have a busy practice. I travel all over the world and then to come home and work on a book or an article. I don't know how I did my Creative Process in Gestalt Therapy. Well, I do know how I did it. I was a fanatic. I wrote in the airports, on airplanes, in bathrooms. I wrote at six o'clock in the morning, before I saw my patients. I just had to do that book. After awhile, you run out of juice.

Robert: Yes. When I write, I block off time on my schedule. Working at the university, I have that permission. They like publishing. It looks good for the university for me to publish.

Joseph: Well, you're lucky. I remember when I was associate professor at a college, having a full-time teaching job, I would take at least five weeks off every summer just to write and paint. I remember being on the Cape with my little girls and my wife, running around on the beach, playing, painting, having a drink, writing, and going out to dinner. It was a wonderful life. I miss it. I think I have to stimulate me to carve out more time. I make enough money that I should be able to plan that.

Robert: My wife is in private practice and she keeps telling me, "Bob, you ought to quit the university. You can have a full-time practice in a month." I say, "I don't want a full-time private practice." That would interfere with other things that I'm interested in doing.

Joseph: Exactly right. I think that if I couldn't teach and if I couldn't take the time to be with people like yourself, my work would be shallow and meaningless. We have to help each other, to learn from each other. I think you are lucky to have that opportunity.

Robert: I'll tell the university you said that! I feel that I have covered most of the things I'm interested in. Are there some more things that you would like to talk about?

Joseph: I'm thinking about being creative, but I'm not quite sure what I want to say about it except that it seems so important that I said a lot about it in my book. We could talk about training some more. I've had some thoughts about if I were to have my own Joseph training program, what would I teach, or what would be the order in which I would teach?

Robert: What would you teach?

Joseph: Well, I was thinking that I would break a group of people into triads; you know how we do that. I would focus on the observer, not on the therapist. I would make the observation the most important skill. I would praise the observer. I would evaluate observation and the basic skill of attending to phenomenological data. And only then, once the therapists learn how to observe well, would I teach about intervening beyond the intervention of seeing "what is." I would elevate "what is" to the highest post, the highest level of goodness in training psychotherapists. I would make people do it for weeks, just for them to tell me what is, what they see, what they hear, and how they experience me, and not one word about my trying something or doing an experiment. So, I think I've come full circle. Ten years ago, I loved the experiment and I emphasized the experiment. Now I'm emphasizing the phenomenology of awareness. I think that I just assumed that everyone had the kind of phenomenological keenness that I had, so that I could build the experiment. Of course, it had to have some foundation, and people really don't see or hear. That's one thought I've had about training. Basically, the trainee would respond with a "what is" statement: "You're creasing your forehead, your mouth looks relaxed, your eyes are on me, and so on." I think that's why Fritz says Gestalt therapy is an awareness of the here and now. You can see how he would think that way.

Robert: What else would you do in the Joseph training program?

Joseph: Unlike the slave driving that we do in the institute, I would have field trips. During the first segment in the Intensive, when the students are here in Cleveland for a month, I would have field trips to the Natural History Museum, to the Cleveland Art Museum, to the Cleveland Institute of Art, to the Cleveland Orchestra, with specific thematic assignments. I would sit two students in front of a painting and say to them, "Write down five or six pages of what you see in that picture." I have made myself do that. I just did that about six months ago, and I got off on it, Bob. I started looking at that sucker and I couldn't stop writing. It was like a seventeenth-century painting of a mother, father, and a child with a dog. It was incredible what I made myself see. So, one piece of the process was just to see it. The other piece of the process is to find a language for it. For example, the child is looking up at her mother with a kind of puzzled look, or a loving look, or a look of admiration, and the child is searching for a language. What kind of a look is that? And we follow that process through again and again.

Robert: You do that differently than one would with the TAT cards? Like, what does this mean? Right?

Joseph: Right. I just want to see the pure thing that's there, just a pure thing. I think I'm fascinated with that because, when I was hiding in the cellars of Europe while the bombs were coming down, the only self-support I had were my eyes. I couldn't scream or cry, because I would draw attention to myself, but I could always look around: look at that woman going crazy; look at the darkness; look at the candles. I took in and told myself what I was seeing. Possibly that was a way of surviving.

Robert: Could you do the same thing with your ears and the symphony?

Joseph: Oh, yes. Sure.

Robert: Write down what you hear?

Joseph: Absolutely. I start writing during the program. I start writing poetry. I get so quickly stimulated that if I can't put it out, I feel like I'm going to burst.

Robert: Yes, you have to retroflect to keep that in.

Joseph: Absolutely, or I would start pacing the aisles or something like that.

Robert: So, you get stimulated and energized by that?

Joseph: Well, it's just incredible to see and hear. Right now, for instance, for me to take you in is better than a piece of chocolate--better than chocolate chip ice cream.

Robert: That's interesting. I'm going to try some of those ideas in my training group. I will let you know what happens. I do the triads. I haven't done that much focusing on the role of the observer.

Joseph: See, I knew that. I knew that, and what I would say to the therapist is, "Now watch how much your observer can see. If you can see this much, you won't have any trouble in making an intervention." An intervention is not something that is formed in your head that you have to think up, an intervention comes from what is right there in front of you.

Robert: My experience is if two people volunteer in my training group, one to be the therapist and one to be the patient, that the group typically sees more than the therapist does.

Joseph: Of course, just say, "The two of you--you crossed your leg and you crossed your leg." They say, "I don't remember crossing my leg."

Robert: Yes, we could videotape that and they could play it back.

Joseph: Yes, we are using more and more video-tape now.

Robert: I would like to come to that Joseph training model.

Joseph: Okay, I will let you know in my next life.

Robert: I was trained by Simkin. I would get back out there once in a while for a "tune-up." When he died, I hadn't seen him for several years, I thought, "What am I going to do?" So I wrote to Erv Polster, whom I had met a couple of times, and I said, "Can I come to your follow-up, or whatever you call it when you get together with your graduates?" He wrote back that I could. I was out there in February for a week with Erv and Miriam and it was great--it was uplifting.

Joseph: Yes, I'll have to do that someday for myself.

Robert: I find I need to get away or I work too much. I begin to get dull. Those kinds of things refresh me. Too much Orlando, Florida. Joseph, I feel finished now. Do you feel okay with stopping here?

Joseph: Yes.

Wellfleet

Life reveals itself
suddenly as
a scalpel,
incising its initials of
shock and
surprise
into my heart -

How can one bear it?

J.Z., 1/23/2000

1993

1977

14

An Interview with Joseph C. Zinker

1996

An interview with Clive Hierons in London

Gestalt therapy is not the routine repetition of stale prayers of sundown. For me it stands for all that is in front of me, for all that promises completeness of experiencing, for the things to come which are awesome, frightening, tearful, moving, unfamiliar, archetypal, growthful. For me it means the full embrace of life--the savouring of all its subtle tastes.

Joseph C. Zinker, Voices, 1974

Liberation

Clive Hierons: I've always found this quotation inspiring and it links well with your emphasis on creativity.

Joseph Zinker: Yes, and it implies liberation, not just healing but opening up and becoming more free, celebrating one's own life. Creativity is a form of expression. It's not just thinking, creativity is a way of packaging, of binding ones thinking into an expressive act.

Clive: I feel excited by that and I'm aware of my own internal barriers that hold me back which are reinforced by external restrictions and rules, and I have a wish to go beyond that.

Joseph: It's a way of breaking through barriers without hurting anyone and yet enhancing ones own capacities, ones own talent. A liberation with good form, maybe powerful, but also delicate, surprising, and sometimes just very quiet, very ordinary. I think most often very ordinary. You know, we are mainly just ordinary, it's surprising when something happens that is totally joyful and inspiring.

Clive: And perhaps there is less resistance if it's ordinary.

Joseph: That's right.

Clive: So, if you do something that is extraordinary, that makes demands on other people to make a shift, then you get resistance.

Joseph: Exactly. So on one hand you have the possibility of too much resistance to ones' behavior but with ordinariness there is always the danger of not being noticed, of not being given any credit. Speaking of the ordinary, most often the ordinary nourishes us and supports us and we don't even notice it. A Gestalt term for liberation is "undoing retroflections." It's tempting when you undo retroflections to be rebellious, dramatic, like a teenager, you know, rage at the world, yell and scream and that has an aesthetic place in psychotherapy if it's not overdone or forced.

Clive: That reminds me of the historical context, of you saying that retroflection was very much the issue earlier with Gestalt.

Joseph: Following the 1940s, people felt overly constrained by the culture, at least in America, and got in touch with the empty promises that the culture made that didn't pay off. Of God and the Church 'saving us' that paid off in millions of people getting killed in World War II. Also, the sense of constriction that we had from our parents that just didn't pay off. They were good at making demands but not always good at supporting our growth. Oh, the other thing was a submersion of the individual to the University, the army, the strict rules about academic requirements, the lack of imagination we were driven by. We didn't get much out of that and then Fritz Perls came along. Fritz grew up in almost the Victorian era, and came along and said, "Enough of this bullshit--express yourself, be yourself." Let's open the door to saying, "You say you're a man, show me how you are a man... you're a woman, show me how you are a woman." Then he would ask, "What is sitting inside you that has been swallowed and is completely undigested... you look bloated, forlorn and alone, you're carrying all this shit inside--what are you going to do with it, die with it?" That was the time of the emergence of existentialism which said that you make your own life.

Clive: That's where the focus on responsibility came from.

Joseph: That's right, the whole notion that existence precedes essence. You're not just born and given these characteristics by God and stay that way, just praying for salvation, because that will get you a bullet in the head.

Clive: So there is something you can do about it?

Joseph: Sure, it's optimistic. Fritz came along and took existentialism very literally. Existentialism says, "You are alive, at this moment you are alive, you are here in this space and you are alive." You sit there talking or eating and taking in the silence, and what are you going to do with the sense of being alive--do you have any urgency to live, or to die, or to startle yourself, or to start singing. That's the origin of the here and now. But the endless psychoanalytical babble about the past, and the whining and complaining about having been injured is often dead material. It only comes to life when you bring that material into the moment and play it out, act it out and make it alive. It's not that the past is not important. Many people misunderstand that, it's that you need to bring the past into the moment and make it fully alive.

Clive: The difference between telling the story and bringing something into the present?

Joseph: The difference between telling the story and possibly reenacting the story as if it were unfolding in this moment. Bringing your father, looking at his hands, how big they are, and having witnesses joining you there in that incredible moment of truth for you. You see how it immediately comes to life in front of you, that's what we did the other day.

Clive: Plus the feedback.

Joseph: Oh yes, the moment you create that scenario you stimulate feedback and that is like weaving a huge tapestry together where everyone has a needle and a different color thread. Instead of being just a cognitive point in the brain it becomes a rich unfolding process of weaving together and transforming the past into a brand new past that has its own electric meaning that really inspires, tries to speak with the tears, makes them laugh. Isn't that great? It's great that we have such brains. Fritz always loved the theatre. Fritz and Laura Perls were intellectuals, who broke all the rules, even as youngsters, They were brilliant, and rebellious, and made things happen. They lived well, went to the theatre and brought that spirit to America.

Clive: They seem quite rebellious but also looked after themselves. I have the impression that very often when people get rebellious they sacrifice themselves.

Joseph: They die for the cause, set fire to themselves. For Fritz and Laura the care taking of the self is an intrinsic part of the rebellion. Their ideas and language reflected reactions to the Second World War and the anger people experienced then (similar to reactions to Vietnam but on a greater philosophical and therapeutic scale). Today, in the atmosphere of protecting ourselves and our children, we think a lot about making the world safe for ourselves and for others too. Acting responsibly, conservatively, without hurting others. That's not so easy.

Acting with Regret

Clive: The issue of not hurting others came up in your new book where you talk about the aesthetics of action. The term that caught my attention was "action with regret." That very often when we act in the world there is a side effect that we don't anticipate or don't want.

Joseph: Yes that's true--and we have to act otherwise we are immobilized. Every time we act or make a decision it's impossible not to hurt somebody, if our action is big enough. This comes from the work of Sonia Nevis that was published in the books of Edwin Nevis on organizational consulting as well as in my own book. Sonia says that no matter how civilized we are, how humane we are, how well informed we are, all our actions have consequences that will please some and hurt others. Therefore all actions should be "made with regret." I think the notion of regret is an effort to never deny the impact of one's behavior. A regret is a way of saying I'm sorry, sorry that I had to do this. I think there are all kinds of contexts, rebellious tribes and rebellious children. You punish them or you keep them from doing something they want to do badly, you do that with regret. At a more subtle level, if you favor one child going to university you may offend your other child in some way. Whether you intend to or not, you make the other child feel inferior or inadequate. You can't move, you can't turn around, you can't open your mouth without creating situations that are regrettable.

Clive: I'd like to draw a distinction between undoing retroflections and what you've just said. In undoing retroflections someone is going to get hurt, for example through rejection. Is this a different situation, or just a different scale?

Joseph: Every "undoing of retroflection," no matter what 'scale,' may hurt someone while possibly benefiting the person. The dilemma is that if we act in the world as part of being alive, as part of growing, it's difficult not to hurt others. Think of how, as teenagers, we hurt our parents, so we could eventually become adults.

Clive: If we decide to run a men's workshop again and we see that as a way of empowering men, that is something we sit down and talk about and work through. We can be aware of the side effects before taking action.

Joseph: Yes, but the talk itself, which seems benign enough, involves undoing retroflections, saying to each other the plain truth that may hurt. Even on a smaller scale just the fact that we are talking to each other with this tape recorder has consequences, has an impact on us. At a micro level, every time we speak we modify a previous thought, we round out or shape a previous thought, an improvement, or do something with it, and that's an undoing of a retroflection.

Clive: The key is awareness then, you can be aware and still act, or you can act without awareness and then get all the consequences. That can be more regrettable because it might have been better not to act.

Joseph: Yes, so action with regret is really an awareness concept, injecting awareness into action by evaluating the action and its consequences. Recognizing that hurt is possible, we use strong, clear awareness before we act and after we act, and there is still regret that someone may have been hurt in spite of our thoughtfulness.

Clive: For me it goes back to liberation, any form of liberation is about breaking out, breaking whatever the bounds might be and hopefully that will be mainly positive. But we might lose something.

Joseph: Almost always we lose something. Lets say you break through your shyness and come into the world celebrating more clearly and boldly. You would think, "What do I lose by losing my shyness." Well, you lose something, you lose a certain innocence and sweetness, the lovely embarrassment that attracts some people to you. If I lose my shyness and become heroic then someone for sure will say that I'm cocky, and a phony scoundrel, "where's your humanity, where's your shyness?" So even if you think you're getting rid of something clearly undesirable there is a regret there somewhere.

Clive: But hopefully a small one compared to what you gain?

Joseph: Always when you inject the awareness, I think you make the regret smaller and you make it almost instant rather than realizing it two years later, it's an instant regret.

Gestalt in the World

Clive: You've been involved in Gestalt for many years now and must have seen many changes. How do you think Gestalt is now seen in the world?

Joseph: My instant response is that Gestalt is not seen, it's nothing. Considering what's going on in the world it's narcissistic to even raise the question. If you ask about Gestalt in the context of psychotherapy, a major text book in America about counseling has eliminated Gestalt in its latest edition, doesn't even have it in there. So you could even claim in the world of psychotherapy Gestalt makes only a tiny little dot. I think though that individual creative men and women who use Gestalt and systems theory are bigger than a dot. Ed Nevis, Sonia Nevis, Erv Polster, Miriam Polster, in Great Britain there is Petruska Clarkson and, in France, Jean-Marie Robine, and Serge Ginger and many others do make an impact. They have an impact on industry, on MIT, and on the White House. One of my former students was the first consultant that the President hired when he got elected. She and another woman I know go to a summer residence and brainstorm on how to organize a fluid, well run organization. That's what you don't hear.

Clive: So Gestalt is having an impact on the world in ways that are not very public.

Joseph: Well, let me give you another example. The President's wife, who is a young woman of this generation, calls up Jean Houston who is a philosopher, a Gestalt therapist, a transformer of culture. She says, "Lets talk, lets spend time talking and developing ideas and see if I can grow from this experience in the White House." At some point Jean says, "Who was an important person, an important woman in your development." Hillary Clinton says, "Eleanor Roosevelt" and Jean says, "Would you like to do a little experiment where you talk to Eleanor and ask her what her values are that she wants to pass on to you." Hillary says, "Yes, sure," and the next thing you know it's in the press. The President's wife is talking to this ghost of Eleanor Roosevelt and she becomes the laughing stock of the country. This is a perfect example that no one is immune--except that this woman was so brilliant and strong. Every year she has a conference for parents, the White House Conference on Parenting. In her opening speech she said, "You know, I've always had the best of health. In fact, just the other day, I talked to Eleanor Roosevelt and she said to me..." This is a great idea, and everyone bursts out laughing. In an open society people can make money by abusing us and our work can be misinterpreted.

Strangers as Couples

Clive: One thing that I was impressed with in the first morning of the Men's workshop was the way you got men to turn and talk to each other. You seemed to treat them as a couple, which surprised me because I think of a couple as people who have a long relationship. You'd got two men who'd only met an hour or so before working as a couple and that was very effective.

Joseph: Yes, the process is very similar. If you are talking to a man and you're looking at the sky, Joseph will say, "Look at the man you're talking to, see what happens, would that give you more comfort to see his eyes, is that scary..." and we're on the way. It's contact work; it's boundary work.

Clive: Is that a fairly new development, I'm not aware of you doing that before and I wonder if you do that particularly with men?

Joseph: Well I've always done it, but I've done it with less skill. I've always encouraged men and women to talk to each other in front of the group. I think I am more skillful in stretching that work, in having the group contain them doing that kind of work. This leaves me on the sidelines, because they feel their own competence. I think you were witness to my succeeding in doing that for a whole two days without getting myself into the limelight for the most part. Even with the acting of a scenario, I stayed on the sidelines other than to give instructions, suggest sub-themes, the men did the work. You can see how I'm attracted to film directing. The men were the stars.

Uniqueness of Joseph's Work

Clive: More therapists and trainers are now offering, or are interested in offering, couples work. How is your approach unique?

Joseph: It is unique in several major ways. One way is that I don't deal with content, I couldn't care less about content. This means I'm not a sex therapist, I'm not a money advisor, I'm not someone who will find a job for one of them. I work on their process, I'm a process specialist and I teach the process. In that way I think it's unique. Not that I avoid content, not that I avoid my responsibility to teach, when there is something that I can teach and that they ask for. What school should my child go to? Is this school better than some other kind of school? If people really want to know they ought to be told that I don't know or be sent to someone else or be told, "Knowing little Johnny I think he'd do better doing this and this." So it's not an avoidance of content.

Clive: Placing the focus where it's most effective.

Joseph: Right. Once a couple knows how and where they get repeatedly stuck in their process, they've found salvation.

Clive: They can move on and grow and develop from there.

Joseph: So that's different I think, unique. Another way that my approach is different and unique is that from the beginning of the methodology to the very end the couple are empowered. The couple are encouraged to be curious about their own process, to talk to each other and figure it out together. You're just setting it up. It's an impossibly optimistic therapy in which you give incredible credit to the couples' awareness process.

Clive: Yes, as I've witnessed, most of the work goes on with the couple and you stand outside and have fairly short interventions.

Joseph: Yes, that's right, because if you make the intervention a little longer they lose interest. It's not that I don't like to talk a lot, but if I talk a lot I'm going to lose the couple. I think another unique thing is that, unless you are focused on pathology exclusively, you will witness beauty in the couple. This is just so obvious, but is often totally neglected and is a unique part of my work. It's a continuation of creative process in Gestalt therapy. It's an aesthetic methodology of psychotherapy generalized to couples and small systems. You make the aesthetics, not as a principle of aesthetics, but you see the aesthetics in how they look, how they look at each other, how they talk, their gestures. They are beautiful and you start with that principle, that they are doing something well, that they have good form.

Clive: That reminds me of something I've read of yours. A statement that if you're working with couples never get them into blaming each other, or arguments, because there is such a...

Joseph: A grand deflection that never, ever, leads to anything good, and you end up scalding them. Instead, I use the notion of first working with the beautiful side, the competent side, secondly looking at the underside, the dark, underdeveloped side, and finally doing an experiment.

Gender Bias

Clive: Do you still work with Sonia Nevis much?

Joseph: Yes, in our teaching program. If you came to us and took our program you would see us demonstrating.

Clive: That sounds so balanced. If both of you are working with a couple, then you're identifying with one in the couple because of gender. Is that a major issue?

Joseph: Never with Sonia and me, with any other female partner it's always been an issue. The reason gender is not an issue with us is that we are trained to see the total system so that partiality is discounted. If we are watching you and your partner my brain might say to me, "You know, she's really bossing him around," which is transference. However, this never comes out of my mouth. Instead, I might say, "Are you aware that every time you fall silent you leave yourself open to criticism?" To her I might say, "Do you realize every time you speak to him he falls silent and allows in your criticism and unwittingly you get caught there criticizing him?" Okay, see how I work it back and forth. Then the experiment comes in. "Well, let's try this--as soon as there's a pause--you say something to her no matter what and don't pause." To her, "When he does that you sit back in your chair and really let it into your heart and see what happens." Grist for the mill, lubricating the system and tweaking it, making it turn over and that's beauty. In a sense, my interest in you as being a victim is just my lack of imagination, nothing more than my blindness. To see it as "She's bossing you around" and really let that out of my mouth is at the lowest level intervention in the whole world.

Clive: Just pointing out the obvious?

Joseph: Well not even the obvious. The deeper wisdom is that you do something with your body and silence to irritate her. She jumps into your silence before being curious about what you're silent about, and winds up attacking you. I begin to spin a systems interpretation of you being violated in some way. That puts the heat on both of you rather than on her being a castrator and you being a passive eunuch.

Clive: And that makes some room for movement. My interpretation of she's right and I'm wrong locks us into opposition.

Joseph: Exactly, and therefore into a frozen position, anger and impotence in terms of moving forward. If I'm sitting with a woman, and she sees your partner as being a castrator and she's feeling critical of her doing that to the poor guy, she's not to let that out of her head but again transform it in the same way, so that both of us are working the same track. That's why it doesn't become an issue. Any difference in a couple is often a collusion or agreement to play complementary roles in an interaction, no matter what the gender.

* * *

Sleeping Woman

My love came to my bed and slept -
I could hear her moist sensuous breath
Quiet, still, as if contemplating the
beginning of the universe.

My love slept and I sat at her side reading Neruda
who instructed me about my hunger for
peace in the infinite embrace of life.
Suddenly Neruda jumped out of his book and
stood above me smiling...
He put his hand gently on my shoulder,
saying softly (as not to wake her up)... he said softly,
"When a gift like this comes to you,
guard her with your life, feed hungrily at her breast,
and most importantly, DANCE! DANCE your whole life with her,
and only her!"

Then Neruda vanished, leaving me alone
to birth myself.

J.Z., 12/16/97, Sao Paulo

15

Lies in Intimate Systems

Spring 1981

A conversation between Sonia Nevis and Joseph Zinker

Joseph: Are lies bad by definition? I was taught categorically not to lie. Did our parents teach us the right thing when they taught us not to lie?

Sonia: Yes, our parents taught us absolutely correctly that it is important not to lie in intimate situations, and since the parent-child situation is an intimate one, out of the context of that situation lying is not good. What most parents didn't tell us is that not all of life is an intimate situation. Intimacy is where we get our emotional nourishment, and without intimacy our lives are barren, but much of life is not intimate.

Joseph: The worth or awfulness of lying needs to be discussed in the context of whether it takes place in intimate situations or in other kinds of situations. Is that what you mean?

Sonia: Yes. The essence of intimacy is knowing and being known. Therefore, it is important to me to know that I do not have to be known, that I do not have to tell the truth to anybody that asks it of me. Lying has to do with a very old and basic tenet of survival, and I know that I practice the skill in many innocent ways. If someone on an airplane asks me what I do, I often say I am a housewife and I have eight children. I practice the skill of not being known in order to feel comfortable in the world.

Joseph: As you were talking, I remembered a survival experience I had. I was 16 years old, and I found myself in a tent in a girl's camp at night. The director of the camp, who looked like he was eight feet tall, walked in and barked, "What are you doing here?" I could not offer a reason that would not get me into trouble, so I started talking Yiddish. I talked Yiddish a-mile-a-minute until he finally threw me out.

Sonia: Because he couldn't know anything.

Joseph: Right. And I felt safe.

Sonia: Exactly. Since intimacy is being known and knowing, then truth-telling is the building of intimacy.

Joseph: It is the vehicle by which intimacy develops.

Sonia: Yes. That is not a simple process. To tell the truth is to struggle. When I tell the truth I have to push myself to articulate complexities about how I feel and what I think. It is hard to tell the truth because I do not always like what I think, I do not always like what I feel, I do not always know what I think and feel until I say it, and I do not know how it will be received. I have to trust it will be received gently. It is simply to lie or to avoid the truth by being silent. So intimacy, which is based on truth, takes a lot of time. If I ask someone I care about--"Do you love me?"--to really answer me would take an afternoon to say what is going on. Yet that is what we need to do, to spend an afternoon on something like that. So telling the truth is work.

Joseph: Telling the truth is the work of intimacy.

Sonia: Yes.

Joseph: It sounds like making a lie, or modifying the truth in some way, is a way of regulating the distance or the degree of intimacy between people. If you say to that person on the airplane that you are a housewife with eight children, you are determining how close you want to be to that individual.

Sonia: Yes. I think we begin with lies in situations where intimacy is starting and growing. We begin with simple lies like, "You're beautiful," or "I love you." As intimacy grows, we are able to tell more and more of the truth. When something happens in a situation where suddenly we feel too known or hurt, if there's no time spent repairing the tear, the rent, then I think lies reappear to help cushion the contact. We pull back by telling lies, by not saying something, by simplifying something, by avoiding or changing the subject. We have to attend to the telling of truth--it cannot be done on the run.

Joseph: It is interesting to consider the lie or the truth as related to time, that we can dismiss someone with a quick lie, but to tell the truth implies telling the whole truth, searching for the fitting words that represent our actual experience. So taking the time is a very important factor.

Sonia: I think so, I think it is a critical factor, so intimacy is hard to come by.

Joseph: You are saying that telling the truth is much more complex and difficult than telling a lie.

Sonia: I believe that.

Joseph: One can simplify reality with a lie. One can make it very ordinary and banal. You are saying that to tell the truth makes a much richer experience. Why is truth more complex? Is it your definition of the turth that makes it so complex? When I think about the phenomenology of truth, mainly truth not as a response to a test question but as a description of my experience, then it immediately feels complex.

Sonia: I think you said it in your question. Experience is very complex. Feelings are complex. Thoughts are complex. Articulating them is very difficult.

Joseph: Then telling the truth is faithfully reporting one's experience.

Sonia: Precisely. And the wonderment that we feel when we really tell the truth and have it received…

Joseph: Wets one's eyes and warms one's heart.

Sonia: Sure. It is the eye of our experience and it is intimacy.

Joseph: When you are talking with me now about telling the truth, I feel very close to you. Hearing you share those ideas with me feels like you are taking the time to tell what that is for you. It feels lovely.

Sonia: And for me. As I said earlier, I don't tell about myself easily. I am telling it to you, and I am very aware that we are taping it for a lot of people to read. That goes against my usual behavior, and

I am sure that it part of my not wanting to write. When I talk to you I can see your response, and we shut off the recorder to clear up anything we need to clarify. When I send out my edited words, it is hard for me to call them the truth. I do not know how they are received or who wants to answer me.

Joseph: It is delicate. I am just learning about that. During an interview, I was asked a question about narcissism in Gestalt therapy. I agreed with the interviewer. I said, "Yes, Gestalt therapy tended to be narcissistic, especially on the west coast."

Sonia: It has to be a lie. It is too simple. It is not a moral issue. We must lie for lack of time and space and attention. Lying is a sad necessity.

Joseph: I received an angry letter from a colleague who was offended.

Sonia: I can understand that, because the issue is more complicated than that.

Joseph: I was being careless with my thoughts. I did not take the time to express the full complexity of my thoughts and feelings.

Sonia: You were simplifying, and that is what I am calling a lie.

Joseph: The truth is not a title of the article, the truth is the article. When the truth is pruned down to a simple headline, it is in essence a lie.

Sonia: You have got exactly what I mean.

Joseph: Because it does not tell the story, it merely attracts the reader to read the story. And for you, the truth is not just an arrow pointing to something, it is the something itself. I would like you to say something about the meanness of the truth, the potentiality of the truth as a dagger. I have often seen that truth is valued so much between a couple that they will tell the truth even if it hurts the other deeply and sometimes irrevocably.

Sonia: The truth often hurts. I have had as much experience about the truth hurting me when I hear it as you have. I believe that, in a fully intimate situation, difficult truths can be told, if their full complexity can be acknowledged. We may grow sadder and wiser from it, but I do not think it is inevitable that we close off to each other.

Joseph: So the degree to which a truth hurts depends on how the truth is shared, with what sort of intention it is shared, and the kindness and the lovingness with which it is shared.

Sonia: Not the degree to which one is hurt, because I think we will be hurt no matter how it is told. But the degree to which the hurt transforms into a richer knowing, a sadness, a wisdom about the way things are versus a freezing out, a protection, a defense.

Joseph: Once again I am confronted with the notion of pacing and time. If you protect yourself in the sharing, you do it quickly. If you extend the experience it tends to soften something inside of you.

Sonia: That is right. I was joking the other day and saying that I know what restaurants were invented for. Restaurants were invented for telling the truth, because two people sit down at the table with nothing else going on, and they have to stay there and they have to keep talking, and they have to respond, and they cannot go anywhere. When I have a difficult truth to tell, I often go someplace like that. Years ago I thought the car was a good place for telling a truth. It did not work in my marriage because Ed is irritable on the road. That was one of my biggest disappointments in the early part of my marriage. I used to look forward to long trips because I thought they would be times for telling truths, but I had to substitute restaurants in order to get on with it.

Joseph: I liked the car, especially at night where I could look out into the darkness and I would not have to feel ashamed of sharing the truth. I did not have to look into the other's face and perhaps see their disappointment, or pain, or hurt. That is why a car was good for me. And I think a restaurant is a good metaphor for truth-telling because you have to chew.

Sonia: Yes, and you have to do some swallowing!

Joseph: Are there certain truths that are better not told, even to somebody you love, because they leave the other person in a position of helplessness, where they cannot digest it or assimilate it, and it sits inside of them and they cannot do anything about it? Even, vis-à-vis what you said, if you tell it with the utmost love and gentleness and self-searching, it is still not digestible.

Sonia: What makes the question interesting is that we take on ourselves judging what is too painful, what is indigestible for the other. Also, it is possible that it is a projection. We are trying to protect ourselves from seeing and dealing with the pain, the disappointment, the hurt of the other person, so we are protecting ourselves. But in terms of intimacy, the most important reason we should not protect the other is that it is actually a decision to have certain parts of us remain unknown. There may be all kinds of complex reasons why we decide not to be known to a person we are intimate with, but we should know it as a loss. There is no gain in doing that. When we protect someone, it is a loss.

Joseph: If I choose not to say something that I assume is not digestible, because the other person might get stuck with the lump, then by making that decision I get stuck with the lump.

Sonia: That is right. Something that you will not make known, that you will have to hide, that you have to live with and not be known. That is a loss in intimacy right there. It is always a regret. It is not an increase in intimacy to protect someone, it is a loss.

Joseph: And it does not even have to be a gigantic event. If I wake up in the morning and I choose not to share a dream that I enjoyed, then it is a loss.

Sonia: Yes. We know how much is lost simply because of the lack of time. I do not care how much time you spend with a person, what it would take to be known is an endless task. So there is a lot lost. But a decision not to make something known, even if there is time for it, should be made with regret.

Joseph: You are saying that there are situations in which one decides not to tell the truth, and it may even feel like it is for the best, but one always pays a price in intimacy tokens or measures for that decision, if not by hardening or hurting the other than by hurting oneself in isolating oneself from the other.

Sonia: That is right--which hurts both.

Joseph: An intimate relationship requires two people of equal power. If I choose not to tell the truth, it would seem that I am creating a situation in which I have more power than you do, by keeping some part of my truth from you and by keeping you ignorant of my truth.

Sonia: Intimate situations are possible only when the power is balanced. Only then can we afford to be vulnerable. So, where lies abound, you can be sure some are weaker and others stronger and, conversely, where some are weaker and other stronger, then lies abound. Therefore, in a family, when adults abuse their power, their children learn to lie like troopers, and thereby try to restore the balance of power.

Joseph: That is how they can maintain their integrity.

Sonia: Because their truth will not be taken in kindly and well. They know it in advance.

Joseph: It is a double bind.

Sonia: Right.

Joseph: With respect to lying outside of an intimate relationship, from our conversation it seems to me that it is impossible to survive in a complicated society without lying, that in a range of situations various kinds of lying need to take place. If my house is burning down and I want to go back in, but the fireman won't let me, and he says to me, "Do you know such-and-such about fires?" of course I would say I do.

Sonia: We are told that if we are mugged we should yell "Fire!" Did you know that? It is because people respond to that, and they do not respond if they think there is a mugger. If you yell "Fire!" you have a better chance of attracting attention, so remember to lie. But in answer to your question, I do not think it is an issue of a complicated society, it is an issue of a utopian society. In a utopian society, where there are not people more powerful than other people, and people want to hear each other, then we could tell the truth. When there are people who will not treat the truth gently, respectfully, caringly, and respond with truth, then there is a certain lack of intelligence in not being able to lie. Lying is called discretion or strategy. What I was saying is that in an intimate situation, we take in the complexity of what the other person is saying, and the complexity of how we feel, and that is how we form our reality. In intimacy we assume it is the truth and we assume our reality has a substance to it.

Joseph: You mean we assume that what the other shares is the truth.

Sonia: Yes. That they are struggling to articulate as close as they can to what is. We form our world on the fact, so when a lie is discovered in the intimate situation, the form of our world is shattered. It spreads. We have no idea what part of our reality has substance. Suddenly, where we had a clear field, everything is called into question. It feels like there is no world out there. I think that is what happens when a lie shatters us. I have found that, after a lie, it takes a long time to rebuild the sense that everything that is said can take its place in the orderliness of our existence, the form of our existence.

Joseph: In the context of an intimate relationship, a newly-discovered lie can disorient you. It is like you have to begin to restructure your perception of your reality with that other person. And, for a while, if the other person speaks to you, you are more consciously evaluating their truth.

Sonia: That is right. As I get to know you, and you tell me more and more about you, I am continually restructuring our reality. I do that as a flowing thing. I take in everything you say to me. I do not screen anything out, or throw anything out, or doubt any of it. I may not like it, but that is the way it is and that is who you are. That is what has happened to you, that is what you think, and that is who you are. And so a greater and greater field, or knowledge, or substance of our existence evolves. When I discover a lie, it fractures. It is like I do not know where I can stand down and it will hold firm. Is it all air? From then on it is hard to just switch back automatically taking everything in. It is a process of getting back to the place of taking everything in. There is just no way to hurry that process because you are building again. It is huff-and-pull and if the house falls down you have got to rebuild slowly. You do not instantly put the house back up again.

Joseph: Or you are lying to yourself.

Sonia: That is correct.

Joseph: The only way you put it together instantly is to lie to yourself.

Sonia: Precisely.

Sophie's Choice

How I long to wrap my arms around your waist,
        rest my head on your chest and weep...
Life is so much harder to live out fully
than to give away.
Join with me in gentle tearfulness: not just for
        the ongoing pain
        and uncertainty
but for all which urges itself to emerge and turn whole.
Stay with me for the long frightful train journeys,
        for the days we ran across the railroad tracks
        to beg for moldy chunks of bread
while our mothers watched and wept.
Join me crying for all the children
        who were led away
        and turned into dust.
Stroke my hair and hold me
        even as your own tears dry.
Stroke me while I cry for the unborn child in me.

* * *

Let's give each other the full measure of
        mourning,
And remember too
        the laughter-mingled tears
        of all the passion and longing,
        the nights of endless dancing,
        the shy, unknowing innocent embraces,
        the pushing and sweat-joined wrestling,
        the moments of unrolled steamy exhaustion.
Let's have the enlarged
        the fattened laughter of discovering
        that we are brothers and sisters,

mothers and children,
lovers from the days of the first garden.
Let's remember the simplest and most ordinary things:
looking into each other's eyes
hearing the soft hissing of pines in mid-winter
the musty smells of hidden passages of childhood homes.
Let's hold each other and remember
in our inmost tenderness
that we are still children
filled with wonderment of things to come.

J.Z., 8/17/83

16

Why Children?

Spring 1984

A conversation among Edwin Nevis, Sonia Nevis, and Joseph Zinker

Joseph: Why do we have children?

Sonia: Obviously, we need children to continue the human race.

Edwin: Our children and grandchildren are our hope, a part of our interest in the future, in seeing life unfold.

Sonia: If the biological reason to have children is to ensure the future of the human race, you are saying that psychologically it matters to you what happens in the future.

Joseph: How do people who don't have children manage to have a sense of hope?

Edwin: I know some people who have clearly decided not to have children. Two particular cases come to mind. The man in one couple, who is 41 years old, has one of the top jobs in his organization, and his wife has a career of her own. Regarding the other couple, the husband is president of an electronics company. These couples are anything but despairing. They are lively, gracious, generous people who give forth much warmth. These are not people who have decided not to have children because of despair or lack of hope.

Joseph: Are we saying that these people express their hopefulness in the world through their creativity, their political involvement, through the arts, their capacity to mentor others, working for social causes, developing theories, doing research?

Sonia: Yes. To care about something is hope. Once you begin to care about something, you are talking about the future. A passionate gardener cares about what will happen to his or her garden. To have hope means also to feel joy, to be full of gladness in caring about what one is doing.

Edwin: I think so. To see something grow, a person or a cause, gives you a chance to see the playing-out of your values and interests.

Sonia: I think you get a stab of joy, you get real pleasure, when you see that you've made a difference.

Edwin: And with children, it is so clear that you make a difference.

Sonia: Perhaps having children is an easy way to get something that is psychologically necessary in our lives.

Edwin: Why do you say easy? It's not so easy.

Joseph: If we had only known what we were in for before bringing children into the world!

Sonia: Joseph, you raise another issue: should we assume that, in making a conscious decision to have children, people are aware of choosing hope even though it is fraught with struggle? If we were fully aware, how many people would bother to have children?

Joseph: Perhaps this is what hope is all about.

Edwin: In our generation, unlike the present one, we were expected to have children and we did it as a matter of course.

Joseph: Today, your children and mine can soul-search and decide to have or not to have children on the merits of their own lifestyles, personal goals and appraisal of the world we live in-without having to deal with social pressure.

Sonia: Was it bad for our generation to have had conscious choice? Did we suffer because of it?

Edwin: I want to comment on your question, "Was it bad?" Our generation operated out of an easy hope, embedded in a prenuclear, low technology world, and we could manage with less awareness. Life is very different now, and hope is harder to come by. You have to make a conscious choice to have hope, so awareness is much more critical today.

Sonia: I think that's the core of the question, "Why children?" How do we get this sensation of something mattering, something that will continue and that we care about?

Edwin: You don't have to have children. You can be a missionary, build an organization, or follow a cause.

Sonia: A child is a wonderful cause, and it's within the realm of possibility for many of us. But it does not have to be children, although children are certainly a sweet way to go about doing that.

Joseph: I want to talk about another aspect: what about narcissism and children? Alexander Lowen speaks about narcissism as a symptom of a crazy world, a world of individual convenience, a world which favors ends over means, a world in which the outer performance is weighted more heavily than the quality of one's inner life. How does one hope in such a world, and how does one bring children into it? Can narcissistic people be "good" parents or "good" mentors?

Edwin: Yes, of course they can be. They may care in different ways for different reasons, but they care. Their narcissism probably leads to over-nurturance or under-nurturance of their children, but we know that, even in such situations, children learn many things and in a variety of ways.

Sonia: The main point I'm hearing is that being narcissistic does not prevent one from being a good parent or a good mentor.

Edwin: Exactly, I think it's a much more complicated question. We all know people who are very narcissistic and wanted to have strong control or impact on their children, or who ignored their children. Yet, those children are fine, complex human beings.

Joseph: For years, I have struggled with my own narcissism. When I was young, with young children, I could not appreciate them as part of our future, our hope. It took me many years to move to the stage in which to give to others, to give myself fully, to be fully present for others became a joy, a great privilege, a way of giving myself away to the world and to its future. I can see in our children the "stamp" of my wife's and my interests, obsessions and convictions. So far, our children seem to carry these influences gracefully, but not without accompanying pain.

Sonia: I think that a person can take many, many things from a narcissist and grow up fine. Even if it doesn't matter to their parent what happens to them, somebody else usually comes along who cares and then the kids manage. What I'm saying is that kids will not be okay if it doesn't matter to somebody what happens to them. It's a critical and basic human need that what happens to us should matter to somebody. I don't think we can develop unless we matter enough to someone else. Something has to matter to us for hope to exist, but also, we have to matter to somebody. I can remember the passion with which I wanted a child. I thought I was pregnant, and then either I lost the baby or I wasn't really pregnant. It was so early in the pregnancy that I can't be sure which it was. I was grief-stricken, like somebody had died. I think what had died was my hope, and it felt like an absolutely crushing blow. When I did have a child, there was a profound psychological turnaround. There was no question about it. It made all the difference in my psychological existence to matter to someone and to have someone matter to me.

Edwin: Yes, it's interesting because you got energized in a new way. You started doing a lot of things after the children were born.

Sonia: Many things started to matter to me. So you can see it's not the child--it could have been something else that did it for me. But a child carries the possibilities of hope, the possibilities of something mattering, the possibilities of the psychological sense of importance of what one does. It is much harder to come by other things having the same impact. I've moved toward other things happening and mattering to me ever bit as much as my children, but that's what started the turnaround process from despair to hope in me. It was a critical psychological turnaround.

Edwin: Here is another question: what is the impact on parents of the death of a child? What does that do to them? I've always felt that is such a profound tragedy. I can't think of anything that's more terrible. I can't imagine how people cope with that. You survive and you go on, but how do you get hope back again. It's terrible.

Sonia: I'm amazed that even when it was not a child I lost, I lost my own sense of hope. It died--it was crushed. There must be a ground of despair in everybody that it is very easily stirred.

Joseph: And so you tried again, and you have two lovely daughters who are now adults. I think of the Yiddish word, "naches," which Leo Rosten defines as "proud pleasure, special joy--particularly from the achievement of a child." Do you have a sense of naches from your kids.

Edwin: Of course I do. Here is how I understand it: children provide the potential for hope. Then, when that hope is realized by something that children are or do, that stab of joy is naches. So I have naches knowing that our daughters have good coping skills, that they can deal with daily stresses and come out on top, that they can care fore and love others, that they are lovable, that they have careers…

Sonia: If nothing matters to you, there can't be naches. But if something matters to you--children or anything else-your potential for naches is great.

Edwin: That is why naches must be celebrated. I cannot stand weddings where people are not dancing, jumping and are full of joy. To this day, I cannot understand a celebration that is not "all out."

Sonia: I guess that what we're saying is that unless we have hope, in the sense that something matters to us--unless we hope with real passion, so that naches is possible--then we are not well nourished psychologically. Having children is an excellent way to get that feeling. People who don't have children have to take care of that function in other ways. They have to have other things that they care about with the kind of passion that will give them joy and naches out of life.

17

Marriage: The Impossible Relationship

Fall 1985

A conversation between Sonia Nevis and Joseph Zinker

> *In a traditional confluent marriage, the spouse is not a significant other but the insignificant same.*
>
> *Laura Perls*

Joseph: Sonia, I've heard you say that marriage is an impossible relationship. Why do you think it's impossible?

Sonia: I think we want to marry and we don't want to marry. There is no solution, so it's impossible.

Joseph: Can't we solve the ambivalence?

Sonia: Ambivalence doesn't seem like the right word. I think what people feel is more like a tremendous hunger for both marrying and not marrying. The impossibility is the huge yearning for it and the huge repulsion from it.

Joseph: Are you using the word "marry" in a special way?

Sonia: Yes. My image is of a sauce that marries--its various ingredients are so well blended that they are indistinguishable. The opposing image is of two pieces of a jigsaw puzzle that join, but the seam is separateness that cannot be overcome. Two people can either "marry" or they can "join." When people "join," the separateness between them is ever present. The impossible relationship is when they "marry:" to be totally known and know the other, to merge and be as close as possible.

Joseph: A generation ago there was a value in the kind of falling in love which meant a romantic fusion of two people's lives. Is that what you mean by "marriage?"

Sonia: Yes. After World War II, which created much separation, the urge to combine and to lose one's self in another was so powerful that it became a ground swell moving marriage in that direction. However, as we went too far in that direction, everybody began to want separateness. And if we have separateness, everyone will want togetherness again. It's the same whether it's a cultural swing or an individual swing. As soon as we get what we want, we don't want it-it's an impossible relationship!

Joseph: Please say more about that.

Sonia: The minute I get the separateness I want, I'm furious about it. The minute I get the combining I want, I'm stifled by it. So I keep swinging between the two. I can settle somewhere in the middle, but settling doesn't feel so good either.

Joseph: Is this a dilemma for every relationship?

Sonia: No. It's possible to get what I want in a friendship. The distance that exists in friendship gives me everything I need. The situation in marriage is not the same.

Joseph: In contrast to friendship, what is it that we're asking of marriage? What is unreasonable or impossible and gets us into trouble?

Sonia: I don't think it's what we ask of it that gets us into trouble. One of my students said that the only trouble with her family is that they love too much. Marriage taps into our capacity to love. That's a vague concept so let me try to say more. The sensation of loving makes me want to get closer and closer to the other person. By definition, I think that's what love is: "I love you," we say, and we hug tight. We want to stay attached to the other person, but we can't tolerate that. Marriage opens us up to the impossibility of loving too much, and we have to love moderately. If we love to our full capacity, we set up an impossible situation.

Joseph: We're in danger of stifling each other.

Sonia: That's it.

Joseph: What does loving "moderately" mean to you?

Sonia: Saying "loving moderately" feels tasteless and unexciting, doesn't it? Most of us don't strive for moderation. We're designed to love excitement and to want everything to be big, dramatic, and excessive. Excess may be unhealthy, but it feels good! I think that "moderate" is God's joke on us. When we marry, we want to get closer and closer and squeeze in. Then, when we do that, we have images of "Peter, Peter, pumpkin-eater, had a wife but couldn't keep her/he put her in a pumpkin shell and there he kept her very well." I've had images of loving someone so much that I want to lock the door and keep them all to myself.

Joseph: Is jealousy related to our fear of not getting the excess we want?

Sonia: I'm not sure. I think jealousy is broader; even if I loved you moderately but I thought I was at risk of losing you, I could feel jealous. But maybe jealousy is an emotion connected to the yearning for excess. That's a tough one and I'm not sure what the answer is.

Joseph: I'm going to shift a little, Sonia. From time to time, we've played with the concept of good functioning as a rhythm, a form of synchrony of movement or dance. Can we say that "good marriage" is the capacity to move gracefully between excessive loving and excessive distance?

Sonia: That's as close as I've ever come to understanding what it is to live with the impossibility of marriage, rather than to try to resolve it. We are always swinging between these two forces--swinging from the pain and pleasure of one to the pain and pleasure of the other. I'll bet a lot of good marriages have just such a movement, so that from the outside they can look like bad marriages at any given time.

Joseph: In this sense, moderation is more a statistical concept of averaging out, rather than a life experience.

Sonia: Yes, that's right. Moderation would be getting it right, and we're not made to get it right--we're made to be excessive.

Joseph: Do you have some ideas about how we happen to be designed the way we are? Biologically, I know that the action potential reaches a certain level in the nervous system and then there is a release: the cell has to rest a while before it can be activated again.

Sonia: There's a fail-safe system biologically, but it doesn't seem to work as well psychologically. People can be overstimulated. Maybe we aren't as well made psychologically as we are biologically. We have to learn to bound our energies, and it is not easy to learn. Psychologically, our appetites are way beyond what the body can assimilate. It isn't even a close match. It's like a puzzle: why was I given an appetite as big as I have, with the action potential as small as I have?

Joseph: So, psychologically, we want to eat more than our stomachs can physically handle.

Sonia: It's even in the language as in we want to love somebody to death! What do we mean when we say, "love you to death!" or "I want to eat you up!"? Trying to find a metaphor or language to express the size of the feeling is difficult. We search for actions that would be appropriate to the size of the feeling, and there are none.

Joseph: We happen to focus on the one side of the continuum, the longing for fusion. But there is also the longing for heightening of individual growth. Carol Gilligan found that young girls develop more with an interest which is relational-an "I-Thou" interest--whereas young boys seem to develop more with an interest in individuation and personal boundedness. Does that get in the way of marriage? Do we have more instances where men want space and women want to be more relational?

Sonia: The old myth was that women wanted men to marry them, men resisted as long as they could, and when marriages broke up it was because the man left. That was true as long as the aspect of male as independent and female as relational was supported by the whole culture. We see big shits today. It's not surprising that, today, many women don't want to marry and many men do. When marriages break up now, it's just as often the woman who wants out as it is the man. That's because, as a culture, we support developing all parts of ourselves much more than before. Both men and women are developing their maleness and their femaleness. A lot of those differences are beginning to mute. Today, everybody wants both.

Joseph: Everybody wants to be both relational and independent.

Sonia: Yes, and they want it very much!

Joseph: Can't they have it?

Sonia: No, it's impossible. At least, if one wants the relationship and the other one's pulling away, we've got something to work with.

Joseph: In the past we could connect it to gender and say, "If women didn't cling so much, or if men weren't so independent, things could be better." Now that we see both men and women striving to develop their individuality, as well as know something about loving someone, we are still not in a good place.

Sonia: We're in a different mess, that's all! If we wanted to move past this, we'd have to say, "Well, if marriage is an impossible relationship, what is possible?" If I were designing the ideal world of what's possible, we would love moderately. "Moderately" is not a really good word here--I think a better way to say it is that we would love appropriately, right-sized, well-bounded.

Joseph: What would be the right size?

Sonia: We would want to be with the person a lot, we would care about what happens to them, we'd have expectations that they care about us, we would want to live with them and to be with them. We'd want it a lot, a beautiful amount. I'm not sure how to say it, but we would want it, not WANT it!

Joseph: But what would we be willing to give up that would make it neither excessive nor too loose and cool?

Sonia: I'd have to give up feeling that I must own him, and take him home with me, and close the door and not let anybody else in. That's what I mean by loving moderately--it's not actually moderate, it's big! But it's not clutching, it's not possessing, and it's not exclusive, encircled or imprisoned. There are lucky people who don't have that excessive feeling and probably can love moderately more easily than those who experience their feelings to excess. If you love to excess, you're going to have trouble--and I think many, many people love excessively.

Joseph: Which means possessively?

Sonia: Yes, among other things. For some people it's not a matter of choice but, rather, a biological truth. I also think some people love too weakly. There are people for whom separation is relatively easy.

Joseph: What happens when one person wants to love excessively and the other doesn't appear to? One partner may say of the other, "I wish he would show more interest in me. I wish he would initiate saying we should go to the movies together." And it sounds like the other partner may love at some distance, with some reserve. Is it possible that certain marriages don't work because one is excessive and the other is too cool?

Sonia: It's possible, but in some ways that can be a perfect combination. The distance gets taken care of, the joining gets taken care of, and it works out well.

Joseph: But that's considered insufficient in terms of modern criteria for intimacy. They both have to be passionate, and they both have to take interest in the other equally, and they both have to be imaginative about what to do in a given evening.

Sonia: That's right.

Joseph: Let's talk about the force of love which is too cool, too remote, too distant. We've talked about the rhythm between these two forces in marriage. What are people like who have a paucity of love and passion? Is that a problem?

Sonia: That's not easy to answer, but it makes me think of somebody I knew a long time ago. What happened with him has stayed in my mind for 30 years. Tom and Sue were a married couple with three small children. I knew them because our children were about the same ages as theirs and our two families sometimes got together for dinner. I didn't pay much attention to their marriage--it seemed like an ordinary, fine marriage. Then, one day, Tom said to Sue, "I want a divorce." Sue was shocked, and she asked, "Why do you want a divorce--what's the matter?" Tom's cool answer was, "I don't like you anymore." That stunned me! It rocked me back on my heels and I've been thinking about it ever since. Is it possible that somebody can have that little passion? Is it possible to be in a world and not have anything matter that much, not have people matter that much, not care that much, not feel the tragedy of the pain of separating, or the pain of being together? The answer is, yes, it is possible.

We see this in a lot of places. I remember asking you once, "Joseph, can you imagine people who lose track of their parents, their children, their brothers and sisters?" Again, the answer is yes. Of course we can imagine it because it happens often.

Joseph: It's like little kids playing in a sandbox. They pour sand on each other's heads as if they were inanimate objects.

Sonia: Yes. They haven't matured to where they've noticed that there's somebody else in the world that they have to care about in some way. I think that people who have a paucity of feelings parallel play a lot.

Joseph: Let's get back to the dilemma--what are you calling an impossible relationship?

Sonia: I'm saying that if love is moderate, we can move between separateness and fusion in an easy way. But if love is excessive, as it often is, then we vacillate between the two--but very painfully. That's why I call it impossible; it hurts when we are together and it hurts when we are apart.

Joseph: Why is it that in friendship it's easy to manage boundaries between people? People can meet and have a good time and enjoy each other fully without becoming excessive. Why are married people not able to be friends in that sense?

Sonia: My guess at this point, and I don't understand the process exactly, is that the entry point into the excessive is through sexual joining. Once there is a sexual joining, feelings may no longer be moderate. Friendships, that is to say relationships which are "moderate," don't tap into the excessive love, and that works well. I think this is why many people say that friends shouldn't have sex because then they'll ruin the friendship. That's true only if there is the danger that an excess of love will be tapped. I think friends have sex lots of times--friendly sex is talked about and people experience it. It's play, wonderful play!

Joseph: It's not serious. It's not, "I love you, I love you!"

Sonia: That's right.

Joseph: Wouldn't some people call that a form of feelingless entertainment?

Sonia: No, it's sex as play, but play in the best sense of the word-with feelings, with joy, with aesthetic pleasure. Maybe we need marriage without sex! It's not uncommon that sexuality diminishes in marriage and stays higher in playful relationships.

Joseph: Say more about that.

Sonia: I think that managing the excess is difficult and painful. We probably marry when we feel the high of excessive love, and then we struggle with it. We don't have the urge to marry our friends.

Joseph: What advice would you give to a couple who are about to get married, vis-à-vis their capacity to make it work?

Sonia: The advice I have given, and that I would probably stay with, is to tell couples not all problems are solvable. The human potential movement has led us to a new romanticism, a new way of achieving heaven. Heaven used to be achievable through projection and investing the other person with all kinds of wonderful characteristics: "He's so wonderful" or "She's so gorgeous." Now we have a new way to get to heaven: "We're going to get our process right. We're going to get in touch with all parts of ourselves. We're going to get to know all of the other." I don't think heaven can be reached on earth.

Joseph: Do you mean that people ought to be satisfied with their marriages even though they have problems?

Sonia: No. I mean that people ought to be dissatisfied with their marriage if they have problems. I mean that we will be satisfied and dissatisfied.

Joseph: That we should expect to be both satisfied and dissatisfied?

Sonia: No. I think we ought to strive hard to be satisfied. I want heaven, you want heaven, and if we're dissatisfied it's not heaven. An awareness that we're going to be dissatisfied does not lead to satisfaction. It's simply how it is.

c
b
a
?

Titles From The GestaltPress

ORGANIZATIONAL CONSULTING: A NEW APPROACH TO CONTACT AND RESISTANCE
Gordon Wheeler
GESTALT RECONSIDERED: A NEW APPROACH TO CONTACT AND RESISTANCE
Gordon Wheeler
THE NEUROTIC BEHAVIOR OF ORGANIZATIONS
Uri Merry and George I. Brown
GESTALT THERAPY: PERSPECTIVES AND APPLICATIONS
Edwin C. Nevis
THE COLLECTIVE SILENCE: GERMAN IDENTITY AND THE LEGACY OF SHAME
Barbara Heimannsberg and Christopher J. Schmidt
COMMUNITY AND CONFLUENCE: UNDOING THE CLENCH OF OPPRESSION
Philip Lichtenberg
BECOMING A STEPFAMILY
Patricia Papernow
ON INTIMATE GROUND: A GESTALT APPROACH TO WORKING WITH COUPLES
Gordon Wheeler and Stephanie Backman
BODY PROCESS: WORKING WITH THE BODY IN PSYCHOTHERAPY
James I. Kepner
HERE, NOW, NEXT: PAUL GOODMAN AND THE ORIGNS OF GESTALT THERAPY
Taylor Stoehr
CRAZY HOPE & FINITE EXPERIENCE
Paul Goodman and Taylor Stoehr
IN SEARCH OF GOOD FORM: GESTALT THERAPY WITH COUPLES AND FAMILIES
Joseph C. Zinker
THE VOICE OF SHAME: SILENCE AND CONNECTION IN PSYCHOTHERAPY
Robert G. Lee and Gordon Wheeler
HEALING TASKS: PSYCHOTHERAPY WITH ADULT SURVIVORS OF CHILDHOOD ABUSE
James I. Kepner
ADOLESCENCE: PSYCHOTHERAPY AND THE EMERGENT SELF
Mark McConville
GETTING BEYOND SOBRIETY: CLINICAL APPROACHES TO LONG-TERM RECOVERY
Michael Clemmens
INTENTIONAL REVOLUTIONS: A SEVEN-POINT STRATEGY FOR TRANSFORMING YOUR ORGANIZATION
Edwin C. Nevis, James Lancourt and Helen G. Vassallo
IN SEARCH OF THE SELF: BEYOND INDIVIDUALISM IN WORKING WITH PEOPLE
Gordon Wheeler
THE HEART OF DEVELOPMENT: GESTALT APPROACHES TO WORKING WITH CHILDREN, ADOLESCENTS, AND THEIR WORLDS
Mark McConville and Gordon Wheeler
BACK TO THE BEANSTALK: ENCHANTMENT & REALITY FOR COUPLES
Judith R. Brown
THE DREAMER AND THE DREAM: ESSAYS AND REFLECTIONS IN GESTALT THERAPY
Rainette Eden Fantz and Arthur Roberts
GESTALT THERAPY--A NEW PARADIGM: ESSAYS IN GESTALT THEORY AND METHOD
Sylvia Fleming Crocker
THE UNFOLDING SELF
Jean-Marie Robine